BROTHERS IN ARMS

Camino Ignaciano

Brendan McManus SJ
with James Fullam

Published by Messenger Publications, 2023

Copyright © Brendan McManus SJ, 2023

The right of Brendan McManus SJ to be identified as the author of
the Work has been asserted by him in accordance with the Copyright
and Related Rights Act, 2000.

ISBN: 978-1-78812-614-4

Typeset in Adobe Garamond Pro Regular
Printed by Hussar Books

Messenger Publications,
37 Leeson Place, Dublin D02 E5V0
vwww.messenger.ie

Dedication

For my constant companion and
fellow pilgrim, James
In memory of my uncle Frank Rogers, RIP

Contents

Introduction

Ignatius Loyola, from the Basque Country in Spain, was a Camino pilgrim back in the sixteenth century. In 1522 he cast off the trappings of his old life; being from minor nobility he had trained first as a courtier and then as a soldier, and was vain and arrogant. A serious battle injury made him reassess his life and priorities. He wanted something radically different and opted for a life on the road. He then limped around Europe as a poor beggar, trying to discover what God wanted for him. Determined to give himself to God completely, he threw himself heart and soul into the pilgrim experience, and, to his surprise, found himself having to relearn everything. It was a process of 'being taught like a child by a teacher', which would take over ten years and bring him on many journeys, including to Manresa and, eventually, Rome. Initially he had to learn about the freedom to let go of his own agenda and how to moderate his passions, but it was the freedom to follow the path that God revealed that was the great insight that he learned on the road.

That first pilgrim journey in 1522, from his home place, Loyola, to Manresa some 500km away, was the most significant. Throwing himself into the pilgrim lifestyle, Ignatius learned how to curtail his ascetic excesses, how to identify the voice of God, and how to live a more balanced life. Much of the raw material for his famous Spiritual Exercises came from this period, from reflecting on his pilgrim experience and shaping it into 'exercises' for others to follow. His own itinerant experiences, which often involved discerning between two pathways (e.g. the famous 'Moor' incident, where he had to decide whether to angrily pursue the 'irreverent Moor' or not), helps others to identify what influences our decisions negatively (e.g. strong emotions), and how to get free in order to make good choices. Ignatius would come to call this discernment: the ability to look within oneself for good and bad motivations (the movement of good and bad 'spirits'), and, in making better decisions, move towards where God is leading.

Pilgrimage is the ultimate teacher about letting go of our own plans and will, as we have to be flexible and adapt to what God wants. It's a kind of purification of the ego and selfish desires to become a more open and compassionate person. Essential to this discernment or making good choices is spiritual freedom, or 'indifference' in Ignatian language; it has to be experienced rather than rationalised about.

This iconic walk of Ignatius from Loyola to Manresa has been shaped into the Camino Ignaciano[1] in recent years, with signposts, hostels and a guidebook and website. The year 2022 was the 500-year anniversary of Ignatius walking this route, so I was keen to do the walk, especially as I was already in Spain on a course in the Jesuit retreat house in Manresa, Catalonia. I had already walked the first quarter of the route in 2015 when an injury prevented me from continuing,[2] and I always wanted to go back to Logroño and pick up where I had left off. Knowing that this route was not well known and had few pilgrims on it, I was looking for some company and had already unsuccessfully approached a few friends.

About two years previously I had had a message from the Jesuit Curia in Dublin that a Dublin man, James Fullam, had been in touch wanting to know about the Ignatian Camino. He was a keen Camino walker, having done the French route several times. He became interested in Ignatius on the

---

1   The details of the Camino route, stages, accommodation and spirituality are given in the website https://caminoignaciano.org/en /, and the guidebook by Irriberri and Lowney, https://gcloyola.com /guias/2941-guide-to-the-camino-ignaciano-9788427140110.html.
2   See my book *The Way to Manresa* for the story of this journey: https://www.messenger.ie/product/the-way-to-manresa-discoveries -along-the-ignatian-camino/.

3

Santiago Camino in 2018, when an Anglican pilgrim explained the Camino Ignaciano to him over several hours one night in a hostel. The Jesuit Curia office had thought that I would be the ideal person to talk to him. We met in the Jesuit house in Gardiner Street, north Dublin, in 2019, and had a good chat over coffee. He was refreshingly open about his life as a taxi driver, his membership of AA and his journey of overcoming alcohol addiction. He spoke passionately about his love for the Camino de Santiago, which he had walked several times, and raising money for local charities. As a former soldier he was intrigued by the fact that Ignatius had been wounded in a battle, and he had read up quite a bit on him.

James was very clear that he wanted to walk the Ignatian Camino in the footsteps of Ignatius to get to know more about him, and he wanted me to accompany him on the walk. I usually lead group pilgrimages or walk Caminos alone, but while planning to walk the less-travelled Camino Ignaciano in 2022, I realised I would appreciate the company. The Camino Ignaciano is not well known and has few pilgrims, and it actually goes in the opposite direction from the main Santiago routes. As well as being company for each other, I could help explain Ignatius's famous Exercises through the experience of being in the actual places. I sent James a copy of Ignatius's autobiography,[3] which he devoured. We kept in touch by phone over the next two years and gradually a plan began to fall into place. As I had already completed the first section, Loyola to Logroño, we agreed to meet in Logroño, about one quarter of the way into the route. He would begin in Loyola with his nephew, David, over a week earlier and we would meet on 7 June, at which point his nephew would return home. It was a bit late in the summer which meant that temperatures would be higher (in fact there was a heatwave during that time), but the timing worked for both of us. We kept in constant contact about dates, equipment, guidebooks and planning. It was definitely going to happen.

Though we didn't explicitly plan it, we ended up doing a version of the Spiritual Exercises together along the way. This was very appropriate on the Ignatian Camino and especially during the Ignatian 500th anniversary year. There is a long tradition of adapting the Exercises for times, places and

---

3 Joseph Tylenda, *A pilgrim's journey: the autobiography of Ignatius of Loyola*, San Francisco, CA: Ignatius Press, 2001. https://www.worldcat.org/title/pilgrims-journey-the-autobiography-of-ignatius-of-loyola/oclc/47810518

persons, known as Annotation 18,[4] and nowhere was this more apt than on this walking pilgrimage, which necessarily involved sharing life and faith. Usually something would come up sparked by an experience we had, like making a bus with seconds to spare, and then reflecting together about the relationship between grace and human action. Often, I would send James a theme taken from the Spiritual Exercises,[5] such as the Ignatian 'Principle and Foundation', on his phone, which he would work on alone, and then we would meet later and talk about it. What was providential was the way life threw up situations that the Exercises spoke to and about which they provided some wisdom. The result was an ongoing conversation about life and faith, shaped by the experience of Ignatius, which became this book.

---

4 Ignatius encouraged the adaptation of the Exercises to meet the needs of people in all walks of life. The 18th annotation is an abridged version of the Exercises customised to individual needs, a 'retreat in daily life'. *Spiritual Exercises*, 18.

5 David L. Fleming, *Draw Me into Your Friendship—The Spiritual Exercises: A Literal Translation and a Contemporary Reading*, St Louis, MO: Institute of Jesuit Sources, 1996.

Chapter 1

Launched into it
in Logroño

Packing my backpack in Manresa retreat house in Catalonia, where I had spent some weeks on a Jesuit course, I realised it would be several weeks before we reached this same place again at the end of the Camino. A familiar thrill of excitement ran through me: on the Camino Ignaciano, in the footsteps of Ignatius in the 500th anniversary year – what a combination! On the first of some very early mornings, I was on the 6.20am train into Barcelona. I watched it filling up with commuters on their way to work as I munched through my tomato and cheese sandwich. The towering Montserrat mountain range outside the window provided a dramatic backdrop but none of the commuters seemed to notice it.

Later, while on the high-speed train from Barcelona to Logroño, where I had arranged to meet James, I got news of my uncle's death back at home. I was close to him and so I had a dilemma – to go home for the funeral or not. My initial reaction was that I would not go. I was already committed at this point, deep into northern Spain, with my friend James waiting for me. I rationalised that if I had received the news a few hours earlier in Barcelona, I could have easily got home connections-wise. I also reasoned that I wouldn't be able to get home in time for the funeral, that it would be expensive, and that it would definitely impact the Camino plans.

> **Reflection point:** Discernment is trying to make a good decision based on the situation in which one finds oneself. The first level of decision-making revolves around the pros and cons, the reasons for and against a decision. Situations are complex and often fluid with many factors in play. Here I was trying to make the best decision possible in the context. There is an element of reflection, of creating space and trying to review the decision from different points of view. The process does take some time, though, and can't be rushed.

I later checked in to the Jesuit community in Logroño, having emailed them in advance. They had warned me that the community was closing down and that the place was in a bit of a mess. There was a good welcome, however, and the simple, hot room without air conditioning was the perfect introduction to Camino life. I had lunch with the community and spent some time chatting to them, as I knew one of them from my previous visit (José Ignacio, who had helped me with my injury in 2015) and we knew a number of Jesuits in common. It is always lovely to be able to step into a Jesuit community virtually anywhere in the world and establish rapport like a family.

Meanwhile, James and his nephew, David, had already been through a gruelling week before arriving to meet me in Logroño. They had started in Loyola, the birthplace of Ignatius, and though the first stage was relatively easy, on the second day they had to climb through the Aizkorri mountain range (I had been injured some years before early on that same stage). The Biozkornia mountain pass was almost a 1,000-metre climb, made more difficult by the intense heatwave that Spain was experiencing. They had run out of water and had struggled through 40-degree heat, becoming dehydrated and suffering from heat exhaustion. James had collapsed at one point and David had to run for help.

The next day they had to dig deep and pray hard to Ignatius on stage 3 (James prayed for help in the Arantzazu shrine early that morning to get through the day), which was another 600-metre ascent through the Elorrola mountain pass, where they ran out of water again. The five remaining stages were somewhat easier, and staying in Navarrette, where Ignatius himself had lived, boosted their spirits. While they were in good form arriving in Logroño to meet me, there was no doubt that they had been severely tested and had already lived a significant pilgrimage experience.

That afternoon I went to meet James and David, who was heading home the next day. Excited, I imagined that we would be planning the following day's walk together and getting into Camino mode, discussing distances, accommodation and food. James and I found each other almost immediately near the cathedral of Santa María de la Redonda in the centre of the city. It was easy to recognise a fellow hiker and the Irish face was unmistakable. We hadn't spoken for more than a few minutes before he drew me in and told me conspiratorially that his nephew David, still on his way down from the room, had been going through a tough time. The week-long Camino experience with James had helped him greatly but he needed some help and advice about going home. To my surprise, James had told him that I would be able to sort him out.

I wasn't expecting this development, but almost immediately, James had introduced me to David and left us alone. We found a café off the main square and launched straight into a spiritual direction-style conversation, talking about life, decisions and God. It was one of those Camino moments: I knew that I had only this one brief time of encounter, as he was going home the next day. There was no time for trivialities, so we dived right into the deep end about his life, issues and decisions. I hardly remember eating the food as we had a very focused conversation about his choices and the pressing decisions that he would have to make on his return. Again, I knew that I had to drive this to get to the important issues, to put in the challenges, avoid the dead ends, and keep God's spirit to the fore. To add to the drama, I also had to ask James to give us more time when he returned early, as this conversation was strictly between the two of us. I thought I heard the song 'Perfect Day' on the music system, which was ironic. It was a blistering pace of real encounter and truth speaking, and I felt privileged to be taken into someone's confidence so quickly and trusted with such sensitive life places. The questions I asked, as in most guidance sessions, were:

1. What are you really looking for (God is in your deepest desires)?
2. What is working for you in getting this desire met (consolation)?
3. What is not working for you in getting this desire met (desolation)?
4. What do you have to do to get there (discernment and decisions)?
5. Tell me what concrete changes you are going to make in your life when you go back home (commitment to action)?

Reflection point: Central to Ignatius's Spiritual Exercises is the technique of spiritual direction, actively listening to help the other find the freedom to choose well. Spiritual direction is being a listening ear to another, a guide who can more easily spot our movements and unfreedoms. Spiritual directors actively listen for God's spirit; helping a person to gain freedom from compulsions, to make balanced decisions, to listen and to grow closer to God. The director listens for signs of God's presence, consolation, and of God's absence, desolation, and helps the person to see these two movements. It is not that you actually 'direct' the other person or

tell them what to do, rather you help them
to uncover God's working in them. Often
it is a matter of asking the right questions.

At the end I offered him confession, although a
noisy cafe was not the most orthodox of locations,
but he had bared his soul and revealed his strug-
gles, and the balm of reconciliation was the most
appropriate healing at that point. I gave him some
penance to do in the local cathedral and spoke
briefly to James about the next day before heading
home. My head was spinning with the rapid and
deep dive we had been on, but there was a powerful sense of consolation that it was the right thing
to have done in 'helping another soul', as Ignatius
would have said. I was shaking my head in wonder-
ment at this providential meeting and thinking that
the Camino had already started for me, the unexpected jump into another zone. Little did I realise
the twists and turns that this journey was to take.

Reflection point: Pilgrimage is the art of
dealing with the unexpected, having the
flexibility to find God in the reality of what
is, rather than trying to control or hold on
to fixed ideas or plans. Pilgrimage is a great
teacher about letting go and trusting, about

recognising that there is something else oper-
ating in our lives (providence). Reality invites
us to be flexible and subvert the ego to what
God wants. The challenge is towards 'spiritual freedom'; letting go of our need to control and holding things more lightly in order
to bring God into it (discern) and make good
(God) concrete decisions. Normally it has an
element of surprise and providence, where
things work out for the best if you can let go
and trust in God.

David's story

*David, the eldest of five children, was born in inner-
city Dublin and lived in a tenement house for a few
years, before moving to Cabra. His father was a butcher
in a meat factory and his mother ran the home. He
went to school initially with the Christian Brothers,
then moved to a primary school and finally attended
the local technical college. He trained as an electri-
cian, and then as a butcher, but since 2000 has been
a taxi driver. He met his wife, Tina, as a teenager
and knew even then he was going to marry her. They
bought a house when they were twenty, and had two
children. They dedicated their lives to bringing up the
children and have been together for forty-one years.
Tina got ill in 1991 with an autoimmune condition*

and couldn't really work after that. They had a happy life and always had God in their lives, going to mass and bringing the children up to be kind and moral; they have five grandchildren.

However, over the last couple of years David started struggling with anxiety and depression. He began using alcohol as a crutch, though he somehow managed to keep his job and family together. He felt that in dedicating his life to his family, he had never had time for himself, and now felt somewhat lost in himself. He says his experience on the Ignatian Camino helped him to get back on track, though he suffered a lot on the Basque mountains. He hadn't wanted to go originally, but went to keep his uncle company. The conversations he had on the way with James, and with me, allowed him to think about things, and get his life back on track. He felt that he had 'emptied all the junk that was in his head', and had had an 'awakening', coming back different. Since addressing the alcohol and personal issues, he has been much happier and more content, and has a new closeness to his family, and to God, with whom he converses throughout the day.

Chapter 2

The Sound of Silence

I met James at seven in the morning outside his hostel and, after some wrong turns, we walked out of the city together. The route was difficult to find, as all the signs, the ubiquitous yellow arrows, were for the Camino de Santiago, which went in the opposite direction. Then James felt that we were going the wrong way, that we were walking back the same way he had come the day before. Having consulted with the trail director, José Luis Iriberri SJ, several days beforehand, I remembered his advice to follow the trail on Google Maps. Then, ignoring James's protests that we were going the wrong way, I walked him doggedly through the suburbs until that first magic moment when we saw the first orange arrow indicating the Ignatian trail, and the tension dissolved. City walking is always difficult, and reaching side roads, fields and open vistas was good for the heart.

As we fell into a bit of a walking rhythm on the trail, I noticed that we had slightly different walking speeds, and also that James, true to his taxi-driver vocation, liked to talk. Being more of an introvert, I was thirsting for the silence and being alone on the open road. I was reflecting on what I was feeling: unsettled and irritated that our expectations were so different and knowing that I wouldn't be able to continue with this mismatch. I quickly came to a decision and, stopping, proposed this solution: we would walk alone and meet up for breaks or at the end of the day. Fortunately, James was agreeable to this, and it meant that we could each walk at our own pace and in our own way. Within minutes we were walking alone but in sight of each other, past farms and irrigation channels as the city receded. At a tunnel under a highway, I waited for James to catch up and we chatted warmly as we drank and ate some provisions. This new arrangement was working well and had an immediate positive impact on my mood, and James was happy too. It was the beginning of coming to understand each other.

> **Reflection point**: Agitation or unsettled feeling (a version of 'desolation', meaning that we are moving in the wrong direction) is an invitation to reflection and, eventually, a decision. Here God works to help us to deal with conflict and to reach a solution

that respects everyone involved. The process is: awareness of feelings and moods, reflection on what this means, deciding to begin a dialogue about the issue, finding some resolution, and reflection on the outcome as confirmation of the decision. It is a discernment or a listening to the 'inner voice' and working out what it means in terms of decisions.

Having been on side roads all morning, circuiting a military base forced us back onto the main road, which was unpleasant and very hot. With the heat increasing every hour and, as it was now nearing midday, we decided to stop early and not walk too much for what was my first day. We came across the village of Recajo and made for the only restaurant, El Molino. This was more of a truck stop or diner, but we were glad to get out of the heat and have some cold lemonade. On inquiring, it turned out they had some simple rooms upstairs with air conditioning and a cheap *menu del dia*. It seemed like the ideal spot to stay and while away the many hours still left in the day.

Retiring to our rooms, I was conscious that the decision not to attend my uncle's funeral didn't sit easily with me and had been really weighing on my

mind all day, especially as I had had the news the
that funeral was delayed a few days. It was now a
different situation in that I could actually make it
back in time. I was trying to work through it in
Ignatian fashion, discerning the decision in terms of
what God was asking of me, and working through
the options. I decided to devote the rest of the day
to it, praying with it to help me decide one way
or the other.

The main thing was to get free, to try to be
'indifferent' or balanced about whichever outcome
I decided on. This feeling that I could go either way
helped, given that I had initially been against going
home. Later in the afternoon, I talked it through
with James, who, to my surprise, was supportive
about me going home. I had assumed he would need
me to continue, especially as he didn't have Spanish.
After another hour, I could feel a decision coming
together. A quick check on my phone showed that
I could get home the next day with some creative
travel plans, and my family agreed to cover the cost.
I noticed a new energy and lightness (i.e. consolation) in me as I began to move towards a concrete
decision. Finally, I spoke to my Jesuit Superior back
home and, with his support, I had a decision to
travel home and quickly put a plan together for the
next day.

Reflection point: Initial snap decisions often need to be looked at and carefully worked through. However, initial decisions, even if superficial or overly rational (talking ourselves into it or getting a superficial sense of 'false consolation'), can be useful if reflected on and seeing how they sit with us. The real discernment is to reflect on the moods or emotions that emerge, to try to get 'free' about the options (being able to go either way), taking on board new information and working towards a better decision. The after-effects or 'confirmation'[6] of a decision are unmistakable, however, and can be seen in the increase of consolation and positivity.

Happy at having made the decision to go home for my uncle's funeral, I had a good chat with James and, after a very simple mass together in the room, we had a meal together in the packed dining room downstairs. We discovered a common love of music

---

6 Ignatius says that a subsequent sense of peacefulness or rightness about a decision amounts to a confirmation or clarity about an often difficult choice (*Spiritual Exercises*, 183).

and found that we liked a lot of the same music. We joked that the song for today would be Simon and Garfunkel's 'The Sound of Silence', in our walking alone. I attempted to explain to James what discernment was. Using my decision as an example, I tried to explain how God is close to us, very much wants to be part of our lives and, especially, to be brought into decision-making, which is ultimately where our priorities and values are revealed. I explained that this has huge implications – for example, prayer needs to be understood as a conversation with God, having both asking/ petitioning and listening, and it's not just a one-way process. As Ignatius discovered, God was gently leading him along the right path, though it took him many detours and many years to learn this art of recognising the 'inner voice'.

Reflection point: discernment means to sift or to separate, to bring awareness and judgement to a decision in trying to work out what God is saying. Amazingly, God is interested in our lives and is trying to guide us towards the best option, hence the need for listening and an awareness of our inner 'moods' or impulses. One of the biggest obstacles is lack of freedom or fixedness on particular outcomes such that it leads to poor decision-making. People usually need help and support to make a good decision, consulting with others, identifying our weak points or poor habits, and coming to an informed and balanced decision that leads to consolation.

Conscious of my own decision, I was reminded that listening and finding God's will is challenging but not impossible. Like anyone else, I often need other supports, including friends to check things out with, a spiritual guide, a faith community and a discernment process. The real challenge is to put our resources, will and heart at the service of God and not ourselves. I reminded James that the goal of prayer is not just to worship or adore but to do the will of God – to be a disciple and a follower, to put it into practice. Faith is not just a 'crutch' or temporary refuge focused only on my own well-being. Rather it is an aid to walk with God and be transformed by this extraordinary friendship. I quoted Isaiah 6:8:

I heard the voice of the Lord, saying,
Whom shall I send, and who will go for us?
Then said I, Here am I; send me.

James's story

James was born in 1958 in the Liberties area of Dublin. He was the only boy among six sisters. He married Violet in 1980 and has four adult children. He was educated in inner-city Dublin. He began an apprenticeship as a butcher, as was the family tradition, but when he was seventeen he decided to give this up and he joined the Irish Army. He was posted to Limerick for recruit training and was then drafted into the battalion boxing squad. In October 1975 he was Southern Command Featherweight Champion, and went on to be All-Army Featherweight Champion that year.

He was posted to Dublin in 1976, to the 5th Infantry Battalion Collins Barracks, a very regimental and disciplined unit, that he credits with 'saving him' from a dissolute life and drugs and giving him skills for life. In 1979 he was picked to play for the battalion soccer team, winning several league and cup medals, and eventually winning the Cunningham Cup, an all-Army competition. He left the Army in 1981, trying his hand at various security jobs in civilian life, until finally becoming a taxi driver in 1984, a job that he still does today. After a long battle with alcohol he finally joined AA in 2013 and, giving it up completely, has been sober ever since. In 2020 he joined the Battalion Veterans Association, which he values greatly. He is an active Camino walker and a committed fundraiser for local charities.

Chapter 3

Back Home for a Funeral

We were both up at six o'clock for a coffee and cake breakfast in the bar downstairs, but heading in different directions. James was continuing the Camino whereas I was heading for home. My first problem was how to get from this rural outpost to a major city with transport connections. The barman told me that there was a bus stop about a kilometre further up the highway, so, shouldering the backpack and saying goodbye to an emotional James, I followed the traffic up a gentle hill in the morning sunshine. Coming across two locals filling water containers from a tap, I asked about the bus, only to be told that it was a holiday and there was no bus for several hours. Calmly, I took out my phone and examined the map for any other options. Fortunately, there was a train station about another kilometre away in a village called Agoncillo. The train station was deserted but there was a timetable that indicated there was a train in one

24

hour. Meanwhile, I thought I would explore the village, which was still waking up to a beautiful morning.

The central gem of the village, the medieval castle of Aguas Mansas, is in astonishingly good repair. A stage had been erected in front of the castle and the remnants of some recent cultural event hung in the air. Further along the main plaza was the eighteenth-century church of Nuestra Señora la Blanca, which added a certain grandeur to the setting. The overall impression was of stepping back in time, and having the whole place to myself was delicious. I made it back to the station just in time to catch what was apparently the only train of the day, and I was the only passenger. Twenty minutes later we rolled into Logroño station. The lights failed to come on in the darkened train, creating an eerie feeling as I stepped out on a dark and deserted platform. From Logroño I caught a bus to Bilbao, avoiding the scammers in the station. Seeing that I was ahead of schedule, I managed to move my flight forward to earlier in the afternoon. By late afternoon I was in Dublin airport and, shortly afterwards, on a bus to Belfast, delighted with myself to get home in one day, but dead tired at this stage of my unexpected pilgrimage.

It took me a day to recover and to get my head around the upcoming funeral. A close priest friend of mine had already been asked to do the funeral and, arriving at the last minute, I was able to support him by doing the eulogy. The most important visit was to the bereaved family the next day, and I had to shake off my travel weariness in order to be fully present to them. It was then that I realised the importance of being with them in their grief at this sudden loss. Even though I couldn't do very much, just to be present and in solidarity was enough. It reminded me of my own loss in that my uncle had been like a father to me when my own died prematurely. I was greatly consoled at having travelled back, however; even in the midst of such grief and outpouring of love, it felt like the right place to be.

Reflection point: Consolation typically means an increase of faith, hope and love, and acting against 'desolation' (dryness and emptiness) but essentially it is not about the surface feelings or simply 'feeling good'. Paradoxically, you can be going through a difficult time, for example accompanying a grieving family, and be in consolation, as you know you are doing the 'right (humanising)' thing. Equally, it can feel initially good to escape from your responsibilities, but you can be in desolation, not really dealing with things. The key to it is recognising the deeper feelings (peace/rightness), not the superficial ones (enjoyment/distaste) inside yourself, and the direction in which you are travelling, towards the light, growth and genuine happiness, or away from it.[7]

It took me another day to write the eulogy, having received a lot of information from the family. My uncle's achievements as a family man, teacher, writer, historian and adventurer, including Camino walker, meant that there was a huge font of stories and anecdotes from his children and former pupils. With such a significant occasion, it was important to get it right and it was worth putting a lot of work into, a labour of love. I resurrected an old computer in the house and spent the day writing the eulogy. The funeral itself was bittersweet, a huge

---

7 Ignatius emphasises the need to be aware of the overall direction of one's life in order to interpret the various 'spirits' at play. For people going towards God, consolation strengthens and encourages, while desolation disturbs and 'wakes people up' to wrong moves. However, for people going away from God the opposite is true, apparent delights and seductions seem like consolation, while penitence or asceticism feels like desolation.

day of ritual and celebration of the extraordinary life of service and love that my uncle had lived, with much outpouring of grief and loss. It was moving to reconnect with many relatives and friends, and to be on the altar as a priest to support the family. I also got to concelebrate alongside my priest friend, Colin, in the liturgy, and it was a real privilege to give the eulogy. At the reception afterwards, we had a chance to catch up and share further stories about my uncle. The whole day was a fitting tribute to his memory and a dignified but infinitely sad celebration of his life.

Frank's story

Frank Rogers was from a small farm outside Belleek in County Fermanagh, Northern Ireland. It is there that he learned the values of family, faith and farming. The family moved to Lisnaskea in the 1950s; education was paramount and Frank was sent to boarding school at an early age. He met his future wife, Kathleen, in Glenavy, County Antrim, and they were married in 1965, rearing five children. Frank initially worked as a physical education teacher in Glenavy, before becoming a history teacher in Enniskillen. Many of his former pupils described him as an inspirational teacher, always having a smile on his face, yet modest and humble.

Frank was a keen local historian, researching the Glens of Antrim, stained glass and other topics; he knew the importance of 'preserving memory'. He was a founder member of the Killultagh Historical Society, and chairman of the Glens of Antrim Historical Society. Frank was also a great writer; he had written seven books on various themes from stained glass to church histories, and he was working on another at the time of his death. He also wrote numerous academic articles and newspaper articles; one from 2020, which reflected his deep faith, was on the debt we owe to Christianity as the 'cement which has held society together' and 'the ideals of equality and freedom'. He treasured and respected both Nationalist and Unionist histories in Northern Ireland, and promoted cross-community thinking and dialogue in his writings and talks. Frank walked the Inca trail to Machu Picchu with his son John in 2013; he had also walked the Yukon Trail in Alaska with his brother Denis. He had walked the Camino de Santiago in Spain several times, most notably doing the entire journey as a pilgrim in his seventies with his wife Kathleen.

The next day saw me very tired. Doubt set in and I began to question whether I would go back on the Camino or not. I also had a few anxious messages from James who was worried that I would not return. I had just spent four days in Belfast, had only two weeks of holiday left and the easiest thing would have been to stay at home, especially as I was so tired. Again, I found it helpful to talk it over with my Jesuit Superior and to lay out the pros and cons. He made some very good points about the fact that I had already discerned going on the Camino, had allocated this time for it, and I had made the commitment to James, who was waiting for me on the trail. In a text message, he had pointedly reminded me of one of his favourite songs, 'You've Got a Friend', sung by James Taylor. I also had a return flight the next day and so, with some hesitation, I packed up my Camino gear, ready to head back to the airport.

> **Reflection point:** Ignatius had a useful rule of thumb which was 'don't make a decision in desolation'. While listlessness and fatigue are understandable after intense events, it's important to realise that being in such a state means that it's not a good time to make decisions. Called 'desolation' in Ignatian terms, it tends give rise to short-term thinking and to undermine good decisions made previously. The wisdom is normally to wait until you're feeling better and to think of the long-term

impact; or at least to stick to good decisions previously made in consolation. It's important to 'act against' the tendency towards undoing decisions, feeding in to further desolation, inaction and negativity, no matter how seductive these are.

Meanwhile James, now on his own, had continued on the Camino and things were heating up. On stage 10, Alcanadre to Calahorra, a walk of about 22km, he had run into further trouble. He had left early that morning with plenty of water and food as there wasn't any other village in between. At midday the heat was intense and up to then he hadn't met a single car or person on the trail. He still had over 5km left but he had run out of water again, his legs had started to shake and he felt unsteady on his feet. He was praying hard to be able keep on moving as he felt he would collapse if he sat down. Then, in sight of Calahorra, he was in a really bad way and noticed that the backs of both his hands were badly swollen from some insect bites. He came around a bend and saw a police car approaching. Desperate, he stood in the middle of the road to get them to stop. He implored them for a lift as he didn't feel well, showing them the swollen hands and obvious signs of heat exhaustion and dehydration. They wanted to bring him to hospital, but James refused. Instead, they brought him to the San Francisco Hostel in Calahorra, where they got him a room. He was in such a weakened state that he had to be helped into his room. Fortunately, with lots of water and food, he quickly began to recover. Later, however, he needed to attend the local hospital to receive an antihistamine injection for the insect bites. Miraculously, the next morning he felt fine, but as the forecast was for over 40 degrees, he wisely decided to stay another night and recover fully, a lot more wary of the heat and its dangers. Greatly chastened by the experience, James strongly believed that his 'rescue' was through the grace of God working through these Good Samaritans.

Chapter 4

Back on the Road Again

Waking early, I got up quickly and grabbed my backpack, ready for action in true Camino style. Down in the kitchen, my Jesuit Superior Tom was waiting for me. Not only had he helped me to make the decision to go back to Spain but he was also giving me a lift to the airport. I was very grateful to him for all his support and care, the living embodiment of humble service in his role as Superior.

Tom's story
Tom Layden is the eldest of three children. Though born in Dublin, he grew up in Keadue, County Roscommon, before going to boarding school in County Kildare, during which time the family moved to Greystones, County Wicklow. He got to know the Jesuits while at school in Clongowes Wood College. Leaving school, he studied history at University College Dublin, after which he entered the Jesuit novitiate in September 1979. He studied philosophy at the Milltown Institute in Dublin

and then taught for three years in Belvedere College, Dublin.

His theology studies were made at Regis College, Toronto, prior to ordination to the priesthood in Dublin in 1991. He then served as chaplain and teacher at Belvedere College for three years. After this he taught for two years at Crescent College Comprehensive, Limerick, followed by a year as school chaplain at Coláiste Iognáid, Galway.

In 1998 he was missioned to Belfast, where he worked for twelve years in various ministries, including ecumenism, spiritual direction and adult education. He was then appointed Provincial of the Jesuits in Ireland, taking up office on 31 July 2010 and finishing in early January 2017. After some sabbatical time, in September 2017 he was missioned back to Belfast, where he continues in his ministry in ecumenism and is Superior of the community there.

Later that day I arrived back at Bilbao Airport for my second go at the Camino. I resolved not to do all the travelling back in one day as this had been too much on the way home. I broke the journey with a beach stay, a short bus ride away in Zarautz, which helped a lot. I found a cheap room online, though it was a long steep walk out of town, a joyless place at the top of an apartment block. Swimming on the beach that evening in the sunshine, however, was a beautiful ritual that stayed with me. It was a necessary change of gear that slowed me down an created a space to reflect and mourn. It seemed to do justice to the loss of my uncle, respecting the grief process and honouring his memory. It also provided the necessary transition back into the Camino world.

> **Reflection point:** The temptation is always to do things as efficiently and fast as possible, especially travel and transitions. The problem is that as human beings we need time and space to process our experience; we are not machines, even though technology and the modern world would have us think that. The potential for disconnectedness, 'numbness' and not really being present is very high. The Ignatian approach is deliberately to build in a pause and time for reflection, which allows us to experience the feelings, acknowledge what has happened, and fully live our moments in order to process the past and be fully present to ourselves and others in the future.

I was wondering why I had come back to Zarautz in particular. It seemed very familiar to me, especially seeing the yellow Camino arrows. Then I remembered that I had walked through there in 2011 on my Camino del Norte adventure.[8] I had a clear memory of stopping at a bench by the crashing waves one early morning. It was a moment of calm and tranquillity in what was a turbulent grief story after tragically losing my brother. Now, almost eleven years later, it was a chance to sit by that same glorious beach, grieving my uncle, and reflect on what had happened in the meantime. That Camino experience had been one of the great healing moments that allowed me to move on, to understand and help others in similar situations, and to undertake new and different journeys. This was a new Camino experience, and I had a clear realisation that this one would be about helping James, accompanying him on his pilgrimage.

The next morning, after a local bus to San Sebastián and a delicious morning swim, I took an intercity bus to Zaragoza. I was eager to pick up the Camino and to reconnect with James, whom I had missed. The song 'Back on the Road Again' by Canned Heat came into my head. I felt strengthened

---

8   Brendan McManus SJ, *Redemption Road: From Grief to Peace through Walking the Camino de Santiago* (Chicago, IL: Loyola Press, 2016).

by the experience of the funeral and having been away, and now felt ready for whatever our journey together would bring. To catch up with James, now five days ahead of me, I had to skip multiple stages (this is frowned on in some Camino circles), and work through my conflicting motivations. Part of me wanted to walk the entire route for my own sense of achievement, but I had a strong sense that I was being called to accompany James on his journey. This little discernment helped me get clear, let go of my own plans, and focus on James and our retreat together.

> **Reflection point:** Pilgrimage is never about the physical journey, the 'personal achievement' of a set plan or goal. Rather it's about the quality of the travelling, the inner experience and intention (discernment), which is much more difficult to quantify. Ignatian freedom and flexibility are the important things. That is, the willingness to change plans and adapt to new circumstances as reality demands. 'God is in the real, not the ideal', and life throws situations at us that test our freedom and adaptability. In this sense, life is the real pilgrimage, 'finding God in the

mess'[9] and dynamic fluidity, outside of our plans and futile attempts to control things.

Ironically on this bus journey I was seated with another Camino walker, Caren from the US, who was changing Camino routes midstream, from the northern route to the main French route. The relatively rural northern route hadn't lived up to her expectations of what a Camino should be. She had walked the French route previously and had had a wonderful experience that she very much wanted to replicate. I could relate to that completely from my own experience of different Camino walks, especially with regard to the weight of expectations that can hold you back.[10] I advised her not to idealise one particular walk or experience too much, though she seemed set on her own plan. I wished her well when she alighted and prayed that she would do well on her next go at the Camino.

Reflection point: Inflated expectations and wanting to repeat previous experiences can

9   Brendan McManus SJ & Jim Deeds, *Finding God in the Mess: Meditations for Mindful Living,* Dublin: Messenger Publications, 2023 (revised edition).

10 Brendan McManus, *The Way to Manresa* (Dublin: Messenger Publications, 2020).

become unhelpful attachments that trap us in the past and hinder accepting new realities. Unexamined, expectations can become idols that dominate our thinking and take away our peace, necessitating a reality check to deal with them. Ignatian freedom is the opposite: freely accepting new conditions or circumstances as gifts, without being limited by preconceptions or expectations, in order to find the newness of God in current situations.

I was staying with the Jesuit Community in Zaragoza that evening and got a great welcome from my contact there, David Fagundo SJ, who met me off the bus. It was lovely to share a meal and liturgy together with fellow Jesuits whom I'd never met. They treated me to a lovely evening of chat and good company, and even made up a packed lunch for me for the next day. I had already visited the city some weeks previously as part of the course I was on, so I didn't feel that I was missing anything by staying in. I was once again reflecting on the value of hospitality, how welcoming a stranger is one of the great gospel values.

The next morning, groggy from the early five o'clock start, I caught a local bus to a suburb on the outskirts of town. A short walk brought me to the trail, and I had a moonlit exit from the lovely but hot Cartuja Baja on the river. I was greatly consoled by being back on the Camino again, walking out into the countryside in the half light, this 'magic hour', in between. It happens every day, of course, but I often miss it. I was reflecting on these transition moments in the day that are called 'liminal space'. These are sacred moments of awe at the enormity of the universe as the world spins into sunrise. It was a real moment of prayer, an awareness of the 'real' manifesting itself to me on the road.

I thought of this as another beginning, that I would begin walking again and complete the Camino from this point, not fully taking into account that James was still two days ahead of me. The day was a super-heated blur as I walked along shale ridges and fence lines, accompanied by hundreds of rabbits. It was to be an education in the effects of the heat, now dramatically increased in the low-lying Ebro valley and the beginning of the Monegros Desert. By eleven in the morning the heat had hit 30 degrees and I was really struggling. Every hour seemed to be increasingly difficult as I got more dehydrated, despite drinking a lot, and the heat was fierce and oppressive as I continually sought out shade. Around noon I found myself sheltering under a low bridge, only a kilometre from my destination but feeling trapped, reluctant to venture out in the blistering heat and having to force myself to do so. I spent that evening in a cheap, air-conditioned hostel room, rehydrating and recovering. Greatly chastened, I realised that I would have to start and finish earlier in the day. Also, I would have to get a lift to catch up with James, as walking any faster was not an option. My initial naive optimism was all but shattered and I had a bitter taste of what James had experienced.

Reflection point: Even though we can have great ideas and plans, it is in the actual reality that God is to be found. This means some level of awareness of and reflection on what we are experiencing, and then adapting to circumstances in terms of making concrete decisions. This is harder than it sounds as ideas and expectations can exert quite a grip on us.

Chapter 5

Dealing with Desolation

Determined to learn the lessons, the next day I was out on the road before dawn with a head torch, relieved to be out in the cool air. As the sun rose it revealed a landscape of fields and extensive irrigation channels. I walked a straight exposed stretch by a railway and then came across some road works that blocked my progress, as well as coating me in dust from the trucks. Then, miraculously, the detour brought me to the River Ebro and I had a cool overgrown leafy path to myself, peppered with butterflies. I couldn't resist a swim in the river just to cool down and top off a lovely morning.

I could feel the temperature rising even at this early hour, and I had already decided I would stop early and avoid the heat. The song 'The Heat is On', kept going round my head, a very irritating earworm. James, now waiting only a day ahead of me, had urged me not to walk at all that day due to the intense heat (this part of Spain was experiencing the worst of the heatwave at that moment).

I figured there must be a balanced way to do this while avoiding the extremes of overdoing it in the heat or staying out of it altogether. Therefore, even though it was only about 10 o'clock and I had covered only around 10km, I knew the walking was almost over for the day.

> **Reflection point:** Making a balanced deci-
> sion is initially about getting freedom from
> compulsions or negative attachments and
> being able to act consciously without being
> under their influence. A certain amount of
> experience, reflection and adjustment is then
> needed to move away from excesses and find
> a workable mean or balance.

Drenched in sweat, I was relieved to come across the village of Pina de Ebro, where I had a much-needed lemonade followed by a coffee in a shady café on the main plaza. Hearing the church bells ringing I went into the local church to find there was a special mass for the end of the primary school year. The local priest, Padre José, was supremely friendly; he looked like a hippy with his long hair and straggly beard. He let me concelebrate with him on the altar for the Nuestra Señora de la Esperanza school mass, which had sixty or seventy children along with their teachers. I thought I would just be in the background, but José surprised me by asking me to read the first reading in my 'Fermanagh Spanish'. Fortunately, it was one of my favourite texts, about Elijah in the cave hearing the Lord's voice not in the storm but in the gentle breeze:

> Then a great and powerful wind tore the mountains apart and shattered the rocks before the Lord, but the Lord was not in the wind. After the wind there was an earthquake, but the Lord was not in the earthquake. After the earthquake came a fire, but the Lord was not in the fire. And after the fire came a gentle whisper. When Elijah heard it, he pulled his cloak over his face and went out and stood at the mouth of the cave.
>
> 1 Kings 19: 9–18

Then José surprised me again by asking me to say a few words after the gospel. I was put on the spot, not having anything prepared. Thinking on my feet, I thought 'What story I could tell them to convey the message?' So, I told them about what I had been reflecting on this morning on the Camino as a walking pilgrim trying to figure out a way to deal with extreme heat, which was now up to 40 degrees outside.

I told them about trying to find the 'middle way' that avoided the extremes and allowed me to make some progress and enjoy the walk. For me that had meant getting up early to avoid the heat and finishing early in this very village. I related that to the first reading: God is normally not in the extremes of huge noisy storms (tempting as that might be), but, paradoxically, in the gentle breeze. I tried to relate that to their lives, that God is not in the big dramatic, miraculous moments, but in the ordinary everyday events of family, school and relationships. I spoke about recognising God's presence within oneself, the 'gentle breeze' being the small little voice within. God speaks to us in the gentleness and harmony of good relationships, cooperating with others, building good families and a happy environment. Padre José told me afterwards that the children would remember that story.

Reflection point: God is always with us and especially in the everyday things, and our job is to be attentive to the 'small, still voice within', as opposed to the noisy, clashing voice of disharmony. God is rarely found in the miraculous or dramatic, tempting as it can be. Rather, God is usually working away in the bits and pieces of our lives, though becoming aware of this does take some level of reflection and discernment, i.e. pause, look back (reflect) and identify the movements (discern).

Over a coffee outside on the shady side of the plaza I explained the Camino journey I was on with James still a day ahead of me. To my surprise José insisted on driving me 30km through the famous Monegros ('black hills') Desert to Bujaraloz, where James was waiting for me. We had a good chat along the way, finding much common ground in our vocation stories and ministry.

Padre José's story

Jose's life is marked by his priestly vocation. He has ministered in more than a dozen parish communities over the last forty years. He entered minor seminary when he was ten years old, going on to major seminary to complete his academic training and theological studies. Since he was still very young and restless, he wanted to experience the world outside the seminary. Every summer from the age of eighteen he sought out different work experiences that shaped him, using the money to pay for his studies. He worked all over: in a Catalonian beach resort, for a large company in Switzerland, in the mines in Andorra de Teruel; in a work camp in Ávila, harvesting grapes in France and, finally, in construction in Zaragoza. Those were years of friendships, experience and commitments, which he later equated with Pope Francis's desire for priests to know 'the smell of the sheep'.

However, when he was somewhat out of sorts in the seminary, someone advised him that perhaps the priesthood was not the place for him. He left and went to work on a fishing boat on the Mediterranean coast for some years. He had little money and lived alone but had good friends and relationships. Through the isolation he rediscovered his vocation, re-entered the seminary and four years later was ordained a priest. He especially enjoyed his pastoral work during those four years and felt confirmed in his refound vocation as 'a fisher of men'. Since then he has worked in various local parishes, and has just finished twelve years in Pina de Ebro, after which he will go to Zaragoza. He lives with a strong sense of gratitude for all the people who have shaped his life and for the opportunity to shape the lives of others. He has a special care for the many pilgrims that come through town; he accompanies them with his prayer on their journey (as he did for us, texting every single day).

As we arrived in Bujaraloz I could see James already waiting for me outside the café/hostel, quite a feat in the heat. This was an emotional reunion after all we had been through. (Later on he confided that he thought I wasn't going to come back.) I quickly realised that all was not well, however. He was not sure about continuing and wanted to pack in the whole thing. He had had a terrible day the day before where he had thought fraud had been committed on his credit card and he had lost his glasses while waiting in a stifling Zaragoza train station for a bus for six hours. During that time, he had got himself into a negative spin, not helped by the intense heat.

This all emerged during the lunch that Padre José had invited us to along with another Polish priest friend of his. Over a lovely meal James told us the story of his recent brush with heatstroke, his low point in Zaragoza, and his wanting to go home at this point. As the two priests had no English, I had to act as translator for James. I was very impressed that José immediately intuited his despondency and desolation, and set about turning him around by reminding him of all the positive things he had going for him. At the end of the meal, we returned to our hostel with James in a much more upbeat mood. José had told us he'd pray for us every day and that he wanted to see us finish in Manresa, which was music to James's ears. It was a remarkably providential meeting in many ways.

> **Reflection point:** Desolation means moving away from God, wanting to give up, and losing faith and hope. It happens to all of us, but it is important to remember that there is a deception in it: things are normally not as bad as desolation would have us think. There is also a wake-up call in it to turn around our negative thinking (AA calls it 'stinkin' thinking') and get back on track. This demands active 'acting against' the desolation and making the transition back into consolation, which is marked by faith, hope and gratitude.

That evening James and I had a proper catch-up over some soft drinks and pizza in the café below. He explained to me how he had got into that negative state, waiting for six hours in the heat in the bus station with everything seemingly going wrong. He noticed on his phone's bank app that a large sum of money had been taken out the day before and, assuming that he'd been scammed, got on to the bank to cancel the card (it turned out his son had used his card). He also lost his glasses (which were later handed in). He had got himself into a bit of a state, worrying about the missing money. Not being able to contact any of his family by phone, he assumed the worst about everything. This, added to the tough walk he had had, led to him wanting to finish the Camino, and he had been planning to tell me as much. Looking back, he could see how things had got out of proportion, and how he had allowed a negative and desolating spin on events to occur. I asked him what he had learned from all this, and he correctly identified that desolation had got a grip on him the previous day with everything that had happened. However, the meeting with José and our reunion had helped turn it all around. I explained to him about desolation and how it related to his experience.

Reflection point: In times of desolation, people are led by the bad spirit, who tries to bring people away from God and the good. They are tempted to abandon a positive out-look, undo good decisions and adopt decep-tive thoughts as their own. Unease, a falseness and a hollow ring characterise this negative outlook, which, when identified, can be turned around through decisive action, and consolation and peace can be regained.

That evening James and I celebrated a very simple mass together. The gospel was the 'Our Father' text from Matthew's Gospel and we had a discussion on forgiveness, forgiving oneself and others, and how important that was. As a former soldier and former alcoholic himself, James could relate to Ignatius's sense of sinfulness during his time in Manresa and his wanting to confess and ask forgiveness for his past life. I pointed out how that good impulse to ask forgiveness was then turned to the bad when he got caught up in scruples, confessing excessively and repeatedly, which brought him to the point of suicide.[11] In explaining this I clarified that the essence of sin was not so much the act itself, i.e. sin as a 'blot on the soul', the tendency to think I am a 'bad' person, but rather it consists in damaging the *relationship* with God – God has created me good and I have undermined that like the Prodigal

11 Joseph A. Munitiz, *Ignatius Of Loyola And Severe Depression*, https://www.theway.org.uk/back/443Munitiz.pdf.

Son/Daughter. This latter approach allows me to make that journey to where I am loved, just like the Prodigal.

Essentially, we are good people, created by God in his image, though we have a tendency not to live out this truth. Sin therefore is 'missing the mark', not living from our true identity or doing the lesser thing. As St Augustine would say, you need to understand God's love first in order to understand sin. Sin is 'a parasite on the good', an undermining of who we really are, so that you get caught in a negative spiral of thinking you are a 'bad' person and that there is no forgiveness possible, as happened to Ignatius. Accordingly, I invited James to be at peace with all that had happened the last few days and to keep walking, which he readily agreed to. On that happy note we went off to our respective rooms to get an early night before the next day's dawn start.

> **Reflection point:** Sin is understandable only in the light of God's love for us, in that we are created in God's image but with free will and choice. Making mistakes and choosing poorly, which is the sin, doesn't change the fundamental close relationship with God. It allows us to understand sin as a turning away

from God, however, and gives us a path back of humble recognition and reconciliation through the love of Christ. This understanding of ourselves as 'loved sinners' is genuinely transformative.

Chapter 6

The Desert Experience

Startled by the early alarm, I struggled through brain fog to get all my gear packed and get everything ready to leave. Breakfast was coffee and sweet cakes in the dimly lit café with the owner waiting on me. I left a bit later than I planned and the sun was already clearing the horizon as I stepped out into the dusty street. James was still having breakfast as as he had slept through his alarm and I had had to wake him.

Once out of town, there was nothing but a wide open *meseta* or plain, the famous Monegros Desert or badlands. With no shade and just a straight road I felt exposed and kept an eye on the sun rising to my left. I knew that this would be another challenging day in the ongoing battle with the heat. Still, I was happy to be out walking and savoured the solitude. Nothing moved in the arid landscape except for the occasional rabbit scurrying for cover. Eventually, I came across some corn fields, which were made possible only by the extensive irrigation systems that sprayed arcs of water through the green stalks. I recalled the words of Isaiah:

> See, I am doing a new thing!
> Now it springs up; do you not perceive it?
> I am making a way in the wilderness
> and streams in the wasteland.
>
> Isaiah 43:19

Later, I took a wrong turn and was off track by a kilometre or so. Looking at the map on my phone I found a shortcut back using a farm track. Eventually the track ran out and I crossed a freshly ploughed field, which was heavy going. I also had to double back on myself at one stage to avoid a ditch, resisting the temptation to take the most direct route. I was taking extra care, conscious of the trouble shortcuts had got me into on previous walks. Eventually the road came in sight, and I was treated to the thrilling sight of two huge black eagles taking off beside me. Back on the Camino I shook the dirt off my shoes and set off again. Later, I paused in the shadow of a pump shed to drink some water, the heat steadily increasing from the relentless sun, and I knew I had to get to a village soon.

Reflection point:

We all have these 'desert' moments in our lives, which are testing but not impossible to find a way through. It often means slowing down and going at an easier pace. Getting lost is also part of the pilgrim experience, of course, and it's important not to get too worked up about it and find a way back on track. The idea is not to do things perfectly but just well enough to keep moving in the right direction. Discernment is like this, continually reflecting and making adjustments on the road, in order to make slow and steady progress.

I saw more rabbits as I walked along the dusty gravel path, conscious of the sun climbing ever higher. Crossing a small bridge over a stream, I came across lots of small black dragonflies in a swampy oasis among some low hills. The heat was reaching 30 degrees coming up to 11 o'clock, heading for 40 in the afternoon, and I longed for some shade and respite. The song that had been going through my head most of the day was U2's 'Electrical Storm', which seemed to capture the heaviness of the air and the oppressive heat.

I came across the welcome village of Peñalba sweltering in a hollow between low hills. Although it was only halfway through the planned 21-km stage, it would have to do. Waiting in a café for James, I checked the Camino Ignaciano webpage on my phone. The only accommodation available was a *casa rural*, or self-catering farmhouse, on the edge of town, which I booked. When James arrived, we had a sandwich and some lemonade with lots of ice, grateful to be out of the sun. Fortunately, the accommodation was only a short walk uphill, though the broiling heat was oppressive and the sunlight blinding. The house that we were sharing with some farm labourers turned out to be modern and homely, full of bright prints and wooden furniture. Most importantly it had air conditioning and all mod cons. We settled in for the long afternoon and evening, had mass together, chatted and watched a film on television. It felt so good to be out of the debilitating heat. Later, on a brief visit to the shops for food, we couldn't believe the scorching blast of hot air, confirming the wisdom of our choice to finish early.

Reflection point: Often, the important thing is being able to let go of unrealistic goals and expectations, and instead be obedient to the reality in which we find ourselves. Being flexible, creative and making good decisions in the particular circumstances is harder than it sounds, as fixed plans, ideals and pre-set objectives can hold sway. Ignatian freedom is the letting go of these deceptive attachments in order to come to better decisions. 'Discretion is the better part of valour', or, in Ignatian language, discerning good decisions is being humble in the face of reality (that is where God is).

The next day we decided to stay in the same place and not walk until the following day, when the heatwave was predicted to have passed. We were both feeling the effects of exposure and walking in the heat – it really was wearing, both physically and mentally. It was lovely to have a day off and have somewhere cool where we could rest out of the blazing sun. The whole thing was a lesson in 'bodyliness', or awareness of our human limits, and coping with the pressing reality of the heatwave. We had already learned there was a limit to how far we could walk in the heat (James having almost been hospitalised previously). Our bodies were educating us about the effects of dehydration, which meant we had to drink a lot of water continually, a lesson in humble obedience. It was a delicate balance.

> **Reflection point**: Being fully human means humbly accepting that there are limits to be observed in extreme situations. Being able to read the signals our bodies are giving us is crucial; there is a certain amount of healthy stress the body can take but above that the risk of injury is very real. These are all reminders of our mortality, limitedness and essential connection to nature and the world. Respecting the limits and acting in harmony with our humanity, however, brings real joy and peace.

That evening we had a great conversation about what we were learning from this unique pilgrimage. There had been some hard lessons, but it was very consoling overall, and we were doing well despite the challenges. Both of us had walked previous Camino routes and saw this one as much more challenging and also more rewarding. There was something very Ignatian about this experience of limits and careful discernment; it demanded great self-awareness, flexibility and consistently good decision-making, especially talking things out together. We had developed a strong bond in finding a way through the heatwave and this was a great joy. Ironically, though it was an unorthox pilgrimage in many ways, we were living a basic pilgrim lifestyle and had to trust more in providence for accommodation, food and health. Nothing could be taken for granted. The gospel reading for mass that evening could not have been more appropriate:

> That is why I am telling you not to worry about your life and what you are to eat, nor about your body and how you are to clothe it. Surely life means more than food, and the body more than clothing! Look at the birds in the sky. They do not sow or reap or gather into barns; yet your heavenly Father feeds them.
>
> Matthew 6:25–26

Afterwards James played me his favourite song, 'Brothers in Arms', by Dire Straits. It was particularly poignant at that moment, capturing our growing closeness and the ongoing battle against the heat. It was a fitting end to a special day, short on walking but long on learning, and we retired early.

Chapter 7

Escape from the Desert

To make up time and to get out of the desert we took an early morning taxi to Lleida, some 70km away. Again, it was a good decision and our only option, in a way. The distances were too great and the heat too high, so we humbly called a taxi and were transported in air-conditioned luxury to the city of Lleida. As we crossed the River Cinca outside Fraga we breathed a sigh of relief at leaving the desert behind and entering Catalonia. Here the vegetation was greener, with numerous fruit plantations. We got the driver to let us out at the edge of the city to walk the last few kilometres. From there it was easy to find the River Segre and we quietly followed the cool shady sidewalks into the awakening city.

We stumbled across the Jesuit parish of Sant Ignasi de Loiola, which has a low-key frontage on the ground floor of an office building. Appropriately enough, it was the feast of Corpus Christi and we went in, intending to make 10 o'clock mass. Almost immediately we met the parish priest, Roger, who kindly insisted on taking us immediately to the nearby Jesuit community, telling us that there was a later mass we could attend. The Jesuit community was on the ninth floor of an apartment block, a warren of corridors and rooms. Even at this early hour the heat was mounting, and we were grateful to be inside, to drink some cold water and admire the view of the river.

Roger's story

Roger is forty-seven years old and a Jesuit priest. He is the pastor of the Jesuit parish church in Lleida and he runs the Arrels Sant Ignasi Foundation, whose mission is to accompany and serve people in extreme poverty in the city, many of them homeless and suffering from addictions. He was born in this city where he studied in the Jesuit-run Claver school, located in the countryside surrounded by woods and vineyards. He credits his family, with their religious and artistic sensibility, for the gift of faith and creativity. The school further developed the combination of faith, creativity and social sensitivity that shaped him.

As a child, he learned the values of simple living and awareness of the presence of God from his local parish.

As a teenager and young adult he discovered the communitarian dimension in the Ignatian-run Christian Life Communities. Roger was particularly moved by the murder of the El Salvador martyrs in 1989. This event impacted his parish because the pastor at that time, Fr Rafa de Sivatte, knew the UCA community very well. This event left its mark on Roger because he saw in those Jesuits a commitment to live for the poorest.

This desire for a simple life, serving the poor, following Jesus and living in a community occupied his head and heart for some time and led him to think about the Jesuits. At that time, he was studying arts at a university in Barcelona but something was missing in his life – being of service to the poor. He felt called to religious life and, when he was twenty-one, he decided to ask to enter the Society of Jesus. Once he finished the novitiate and his studies in the arts, studying philosophy and theology was tough going. At that time his formation was based in Barcelona, always living in small communities in humble neighbourhoods. He dedicates his life to these three pillars: youth, people in poverty and community life. He is very grateful for God's presence throughout all these years for having brought him into contact with so many good people and giving his life meaning.

We returned for mass at noon, at which I concelebrated. Afterwards there was a special blessing for the sick. As part of the Prayers of the Faithful, I read out some of James's intentions for his family, friends and fellow veterans. He had also persuaded the musician to support him in singing 'Amazing Grace' after communion. Afterwards, I could see that he was overcome with emotion at everything. He had been through the mill and severely tested by this Camino experience. It had also been an intense morning, with the 'escape from the desert' by taxi and then being so warmly received into the heart of the Jesuit community and the local parish. After a lovely lunch back at the Jesuit community, the Superior, Alexis, produced two guitars and we launched into an impromptu singsong that covered everything from Irish ballads to American folk, with lots of the Beatles thrown in. The community members applauded enthusiastically at the concert in their dining room.

Seeing James doing his thing, singing his heart out and bringing people together, I was overcome with affection for him. It was a risk to walk with another person, not knowing each other beforehand, and then being plunged into this intense experience of living and walking together. We had got to know each other extremely well, in all our gifts and failings, and everything was out in the open. Walking

Chapter 6

Brendan trying to find the route in the infamous Monegros desert.

Brendan and James in Peñalba in the blinding 35 degree heat.

Brendan and James sitting out of the heat in the Casa Rural, Peñalba.

Chapter 1
James and his nephew David Farrell on the first stage from Loyola.

Chapter 4
The dried up pools on the trail at Cartuja Baja.

Chapter 5
Lunch in Bujaraloz with Padre José (centre), his Polish priest friend (left), Brendan and James.

Chapter 9
Brendan, James and the Little Sisters of the Forsaken Elderly at their residence in Igualada.

Chapter 10
Brendan and James in the mountain shrine of Montserrat.

Chapter 11
L-R, James, Brendan and Devadhas celebrating the final mass together in the Cave of St Ignatius in Manresa.

Chapter 8
Brendan and James in Cervera.

Brendan and James leaving Verdú at dawn.

James and Brendan trying to hitch a lift in Pannadella.

through that desert on that scorching trail was such a testing experience, and the companionship was much needed, indeed essential.

Yet we were complete opposites in so many ways. James was an extrovert taxi driver from the city where conversation is the currency, while I was a bit more introvert, a reflective priest whose world is silence and contemplation. This relationship shouldn't work on so many levels, but we found a way in true Ignatian style. Central to all of this were some very straight conversations to communicate what we wanted and needed from each other. Then followed the process of slowly getting to know each other, through continual exposure to each other in the highs and lows of the trail, and the negotiation of a relationship. And that was the source of great joy, being able to appreciate each other. We had to collaborate in using each other's skills to solve the everyday challenges of hiking in intense heat, and learning to live together in close quarters. Then there was the finding of common ground, such as a love of music and singing, and teaching each other things: I was able to help him better understand Ignatius and he taught me about the human challenges of modern life. Finally, we had to work closely together to get accommodation, routes and food organised, no small feat.

Reflection point: Finding God in our relationships is central. Everyone is a child of God and has certain gifts and talents, and relationships have to be negotiated to bring out the best in people. Inevitably, this is a journey of getting to know each other, recognising strengths and weaknesses, and building common understanding. There is a great need for tolerance, patience and especially forgiveness in developing a relationship. The consolation is being able to work together, negotiate difficult moments, and make creative use of each other's gifts in the journey of life.

Later that afternoon, I sent James that day's Gospel of Corpus Christi (Luke 9:11–17) and instructions on the Ignatian contemplation method by Kevin O'Brien.[12] I wanted him to get a flavour of praying with the imagination and bringing this rich gospel scene to life. I figured that he would be able to enter into the scene, place himself there as an onlooker and see Jesus as he moved, talked and taught. This was

12 https://www.ignatianspirituality.com/ignatian-prayer/the-spiritual -exercises/ignatian-contemplation-imaginative-prayer/?amp.

challenging for him, not being used to this way of praying, but he gave it a go.

After a very hot, restless night due to the intense heat and no air conditioning, James and I decided to stay on another day in Lleida. It meant a break from the planning, packing and enduring the heat, which was very welcome at this stage. We were both feeling the pressure, James more so, as he had walked much further than me and had spent himself on the Basque Mountains at the beginning. I was conscious now that my main job was to accompany him, so I was easy about letting go of any strict adherence to completing the Camino stages. I had already given up on the idea that I would walk every stage after re-joining the Camino at Logroño. Reality had intervened to invite me to let go of that ideal. We would have to take a bus the next day to make up the lost ground.

Reflection point: Trying to figure out the best thing to do, or discerning, is complex and demands a lot of flexibility depending on the situation. Normally it means engaging with the whole reality of where you find yourself (God is in the 'real'), and examining all the assumptions or expectations that you bring to a situation. Often it can be liberating to let go of these, though it is difficult as they can be very ingrained and limiting, for example 'I have to walk every single kilometre and not take shortcuts.' This is what is meant by Ignatian freedom; having the courage to take good decisions that go against unhelpful inner 'rules' or expectations, and lead to a greater sense of consolation and peace.

Before the heat got up, I went for a tour of the old city, attracted by the Romanesque cathedral of La Seu Vella that dominated the city. It was a holiday and everything was closed but I enjoyed walking around the vast complex that shows several levels of occupation, from the ninth-century Arab fortress walls, the twelfth-century Knights Templar monastery, and the thirteenth-century fortress reshaped by Jaime I. I was fascinated by the weathering of the sandstone rock over time, creating a honeycomb effect, underlining that nothing lasts for ever. On the way back, I stumbled across the delightful Romanesque church of Sant Llorenç just as mass was finishing. The atmosphere of prayer, quiet and peace brought me into prayer too. I was conscious of feeling very grateful for everything that we had lived through in the last few weeks and how God had been working most powerfully. As we were entering the last phase of the walk in Catalonia, I felt certain that God would continue to be generous to us.

Later, James and I had breakfast together in the Jesuit community. We got to talking about the apparent similarities between the Jesuits and an army, a popular myth. As a former soldier, James was very taken with Ignatius and his story, identifying very closely with him. I explained that even though they seem similar (the head of the order is called the Superior General; the terms obedience and missioning seem militaristic), there is a huge difference in terms of how the Jesuits operate and how their missions are received and lived out. I explained that the Jesuit order is based on prayer and discernment, and that even Jesuit obedience is a respectful process of dialogue and mutual searching for God's will. In that sense, obedience is trying to follow the Spirit, and missioning, far from being militaristic, is in the service of the Gospel. James seemed satisfied with this explanation, though understandably he related more to the military images.

Later in the afternoon, we met again for coffee in a nearby air-conditioned café. James told me the moving story of his spiritual awakening. He had

joined the army at a young age. He was very grateful to them as they gave him the chance to develop
himself, and he became a good boxer and soccer
player. Later, though, he turned to drink and his
life took a very bad turn. Eventually, he reached
a real low point. Going up the stairs one evening
his wife gave him a very disturbing look (it turns
out she was going to leave him that very night). He
went into the bathroom and, in a very bad way, he
began to implore God to help him, begging on his
knees. Then, he saw the face of Jesus in the mirror
looking at him. This Jesus was wounded and bleed-
ing, like the image of the Sacred Heart, and immediately he realised that this compassionate gaze was
out of love for him. He broke down and cried his
eyes out in his bedroom afterwards.

Later that evening he went to a meeting of Alcoholics Anonymous (AA) and never looked back.
He worked his way through the programme and
back to sobriety, and back to his wife and family.
As part of his Twelve Step programme, he also went
to the Cistercian monks in Bolton Abbey, County
Kildare, where he spent some time finding himself
and learning how to meditate, which he still does
every morning. Some months later his wife showed
him the letter she had written that particular night,

telling him that she was leaving and couldn't take his drinking anymore. He acknowledges that God found him at that moment and helped him 'turn around' or 'wake up' to his life and responsibilities.

> **Reflection point:** At the heart of the Spiritual Exercises is the relationship with Jesus and the realisation that Jesus suffered and died for me personally. This insight changes everything; realising that you are loved and are even worth dying for is liberating and transformative. Sometimes it takes a big life event or moment of crisis to realise this central Christian insight, that there are limits to our own efforts or ego, and freedom consists in giving ourselves totally to this God of love. The AA programme is based on very similar insights and is very Ignatian: realising our own inability to control our lives and our total dependence on God.[13]

---

13 A Jesuit helped the founder of Alcoholics Anonymous, Bill Wilson, to shape and refine the spirituality of conversion and renewal of life. Robert Fitzgerald SJ, *The Soul of Sponsorship* (Center City, MN: Hazelden, 1995); Jim Harbaugh, *A 12-Step Approach to the Spiritual Exercises of Ignatius* (Kansas City, KS: Sheed & Ward, 1997). See also Brendan McManus SJ, *The Way to Manresa* (Dublin: Messenger Publications, 2020), for a fuller exploration of this topic.

On the way back from the cafe I pointed out that God is always trying to 'find us', and that he, James, just happened to be open at that moment, having essentially reached the end of the line. Even though James had experienced this transformative love of God, he kept coming back to his fear about losing his faith and slipping backwards. As he had expressed this before, I pointed out that this recurring fear or anxiety wasn't from God, and that the key thing was to identify that as unhelpful and from the 'bad spirit'. I told him not to get discouraged on his journey, which was so obviously going in a good direction, and not to be put off or overly worried.

> **Reflection point**: The 'bad spirit,' or the 'enemy of human nature', as Ignatius calls it, works in a contrary direction to the good. It works to plant doubts, make people uneasy and throw them off track. In this case, when a person is moving in a good direction and making progress, it works to undo this, trying to make them question and reverse the progress. This manifests itself as desolation, doubts, anxiety and unease, but it is more easily seen through reflection (the Examen)

or through someone else pointing it out, for example a spiritual guide or director.

Satisfied with a very good day and lots of good conversation, we retired early as we had another dawn start the next day.

Chapter 8

Detour to Verdú

One of the key Ignatian sites, not on the original route of Ignatius but added subsequently, is Verdú, the birthplace of the famous Jesuit saint, Peter Claver. Through a Spanish friend on my Ignatian course in Manresa I had a contact there, Anna María Pijuan, who had promised to meet us and be our guide. We worked out that we could get an early bus to a nearby town (our walking days were getting shorter and shorter) and a two-hour walk would bring us to Verdú before the heat built up. Due to a mix-up over the exact location of the bus stop, at the last moment we ended up having to sprint across the road with our rucksacks and narrowly made the bus. It was another one of those pilgrim moments that saw providence smile on us and had us reflecting on our effort and God's work (the relationship between grace and nature). We had to do the work of figuring out what was happening, realise we were at the wrong stop and race across the road, and God was working in our making it at the last moment. A close call but a great joy to be on our way.

St Peter Claver was a Catalan Jesuit who gave his life in service to slaves in Colombia in Latin America. He was born in 1580 into a simple Catholic family in Verdú and studied initially at university in Barcelona, where he was noted for his intelligence and piety. He entered the Society of Jesus in 1601 at the age of twenty. Studying philosophy in Majorca, he met the famous porter, Brother Alphonsus Rodriguez, who encouraged him to go to the new missions in America. He would later become known as the 'holy defender of the black slaves' in the port of Cartagena de Indias, Colombia (I had the privilege of visiting his shrine there several times). Cartagena was one of two ports where slaves from Africa arrived to be sold in South America, enduring harsh conditions. For thirty-three years, from 1616 to 1650, Peter Claver worked daily to minister to the needs of the 10,000 slaves who arrived at Cartagena each year.

It was therefore with a certain amount of anticipation that I approached Verdú, dramatically built around a fortress on a hilltop, with James a few minutes behind me. The road had brought us through rolling hills, vineyards and olive tree plantations, a pleasant change from the desert. I paused just outside town to let James catch up and we contemplated the town laid out dramatically before us. I let James go ahead while I took an extra detour around the town to savour the quiet plantations and dusty roads. When I arrived, James was already installed in a café on a plaza near the centre. I joined him for lunch outside and we watched village life unfold around us, the café being the hub for meals and conversation. The café owner in particular was very good to us, James having managed to befriend him even without any Spanish. One of the songs played on the sound system was 'Radio', by the Corrs, apparently a previous number 1 hit in Spain. Afterwards we found the smart new Peter Claver pilgrim hostel, left open for us by Anna Maria, which we had all to ourselves.

Anna Maria joined us soon afterwards and we were treated to a wonderful individually guided tour of the Peter Claver Museum and shrine, located in the adjoining building. Next, she brought us to the thirteenth-century parish church of Santa Maria, with its Romanesque portal and Gothic sculptures of the Virgin and Saint Flavia. She drew our attention to the crucified Christ figure, reputedly from the thirteenth century and the object of much devotion. It spoke to both of us in the light of our conversation about the Sacred Heart and Christ's

love for us. In the nave was a wooden polychrome
Baroque by Agustí Pujol, the seventeenth-century
Catalan sculptor, and the altar fresco was by Jaume
Miguel. The atmosphere of prayer and peace that
radiated from the building drew us into silence and
prayer too. Afterwards Maria brought us next door
to the twelfth-century frontier castle, complete with
keep and dungeon, later developed by the Cister-
cians as a residence-palace. It had been renovated
in recent years and had become a community hub
used for all sorts of civic events and receptions.

Anna Maria had been the perfect guide, knowl-
edgeable and dedicated, and very gracious with her
time. The highlight of the day, however, was the
three of us celebrating mass together in the shrine
chapel adjacent to the hostel. The simple but profound ritual of 'breaking the bread' seemed totally
in keeping with the life and mission of Peter Claver
who gave so deeply of himself.

Anna Maria's story
Anna Maria was born in Verdú on 29 August 1948.
She was part of a large family spanning four genera-
tions who all lived together; she is the oldest of two
siblings. She was educated in a school run by the
Vedruna Carmelite Sisters in Verdú, where she studied
the normal curriculum plus some accounting courses

that qualified her for office work. She worked for a few years in an agricultural company in Barcelona before returning to her home town. Not having many options there, she had to resort to sewing and casual agricultural work. About twenty years ago, a Vedruna Laity was formed by the same Carmelites and it was a welcome opportunity for her to deepen her understanding of the Gospel. This practical application of the Gospel as service was eye-opening for her in terms of the implications and, frequently, the cost of discipleship.

Anna Maria's relationship with the Sanctuary of St Peter Claver has always been a cornerstone of her life. The diocesan priest who originally ran it was very devoted to the saint. He taught her and others about Ignatius, teaching them classic prayers and hymns. When he died, the Jesuits took over the Sanctuary and asked for volunteers to form the 'Friends of San Pedro Claver Association', of which she was part. They were responsible for staffing the Sanctuary, receiving pilgrims, and looking after the museum. She learned a lot from visiting groups though sitting in on the sermons and talks on how to follow the example of St Peter Claver. She says that preparing for the major feast days helped her spirituality a lot.

Her simple life continues in this small town: helping the nuns, assisting in the parish, cleaning the Sanctuary and looking after pilgrims. What she admires about *the pilgrims is their spirituality; it helps her to live her faith and to always be grateful. Especially during the pandemic, she was thrown back on her own inner life and came to appreciate visitors more. She sees her vocation as being like Anna, the prophetess in Luke's Gospel (Luke 2:36–38), who, also without a husband, dedicated herself to the temple and receiving others.*

Later, James and I had a simple supper in the hostel consisting of takeaway pizza. Inspired by Anna Maria, we were talking about Ignatius and Peter Claver and how dedicated they were to service of others. We got talking about how they managed to overcome their egos and how we could likewise learn how to reduce the negative effects of egoism or selfishness. I told James about the Ignatian idea of everything being a gift from God and how we have to use our gifts well in service of God or let go of them if they become a hindrance. In that sense, a healthy ego is a useful tool and, up to a point, an important part of being human; however, the ego can also be a source of great selfishness. We talked about Irish singer Bono, as a good example of someone who was able to use his gifts and fame in the service of the world and good causes. We also discussed how the ego can dominate a person and can derail lives and undermine service of others.

I sent James the Ignatian Principle and Foundation, which seemed to fit in with this theme:

The goal of our life is to live with God for ever. God, who loves us, gave us life. Our own response of love allows God's life to flow into us without limit.

All the things in this world are gifts of God, presented to us so that we can know God more easily and make a return of love more readily.

As a result, we appreciate and use all these gifts of God insofar as they help us develop as loving persons. But if any of these gifts become the centre of our lives, they displace God and so hinder our growth towards our goal.

In everyday life, then, we must hold ourselves in balance before all of these created gifts insofar as we have a choice and are not bound by some obligation. We should not fix our desires on health or sickness, wealth or poverty, success or failure, a long life or a short one. For everything has the potential of calling forth in us a deeper response to our life in God.

Our only desire and our one choice should be this: I want and I choose what better leads to God's deepening his life in me.[14]

Later, I asked James how he had found these days and this pilgrimage. He said it had helped him a great deal and that he 'had got his head sorted', though he dearly wanted to hold on to this and was afraid of losing it (I repeated that you never lose God). I asked him what he was going to do differently when he got home. He said he was going to do good things, to be positive and to continue raising money for charity.

The next morning, we were up before dawn and left town by the light of our headtorches. It was a 15-km walk into Cervera, where we planned to rejoin the main Camino route. On a hill outside Verdú, we paused to look back at the town, the light in the tower accentuated by the dawn half-light. It had been an inspiring visit and the spirit of Peter Claver was very much with us. We walked on in silence, alone in our thoughts and reflections,

14 David L. Fleming, op. cit.

enjoying the vineyards and olive plantations in the relative cool of the morning.

I reached Cervera first, entering the fortified old town through Carrer Major. Walking past the tall townhouses crowded around a central spine was like stepping back into the Middle Ages. This street led me to the main plaza with the church of Santa Maria and the Baroque-style *Paeria* (town hall). The remains of the fourteenth-century walls, a vestige of this historically strategic town, made it an impressive citadel even now. Tired, I found a shady spot to sit overlooking over the valley while waiting for James. The view of a fertile plain and the River Ondara was a relief from the barren desert we'd experienced a few days before. As I cleaned my glasses, it was a natural moment of contemplation and letting things settle interiorly after the morning's walking.

> **Reflection point**: Reflection is a simple spiritual exercise; it is like waiting for ripples to dissipate in a pool in order to be able to see clearly into it. The inner depths are where the treasure is, not on the often-turbulent surface, which is why we need time to let things settle. We need to stop and clean our lenses regularly, aware of the filters and imposed

ideas that we can bring to situations. The important thing is letting the 'surface' emotions settle, taking time to slow down and just be. This helps us to be able to see more clearly what beauty is actually present (where God is) and how we are implicated in it, because we are made of the same 'stuff', made by the same Creator.

We met at the bus station as planned and, to avoid the heat at this hour, took a short fifteen-minute bus ride to what we thought was a good accommodation option, La Pannadella, a motel recommended by the tourist office. On the bus a woman overheard us talking and it turned out she was English but living and working in Spain. Annabel was a nurse and was working locally. We were telling her about doing the Ignatian Camino and about how tough it was in the heat. James insisted on telling her that I was a writer, and she gasped, 'I have your book on my Kindle!'. We had no time for anything else as the bus pulled in. We promised to stay in touch on Facebook.

The motel was nothing special, the rooms basic and without air conditioning, which meant a hot and stuffy night with little sleep. Like a lot of places of transition, there wasn't a great atmosphere, the staff seemed tired and cynical. An older waiter who checked us into the rooms was distracted and detached to the point of almost treating us as an annoyance. Getting into the rooms was an escape from the heat and the tedium of reception. Fortunately, they did have a budget *menu del día*, which was extensive and tasty, and we tucked into it for lunch. We would have the same menu again for dinner later. In between there were lots of hours of rest and reflection, brief meetings outside in the shade and the consumption of many isotonic beverages to stay hydrated. At one stage I went for a walk and quickly realised this was just a hamlet, a glorified truck stop, hemmed in by barley fields and a wall of oppressive heat. It was billed as a mountain pass in the guidebook, but that seemed overplayed. Feeling somewhat trapped, I retreated to my room.

Later that afternoon, James was asking me about the Principle and Foundation that I had sent him earlier, particularly the line: 'But if any of these gifts become the centre of our lives, they displace God and so hinder our growth toward our goal'. We talked about alcohol being the most obvious example of something that can take over our lives. It can be a gift from God, but misused it is a terrible tyrant, and addiction is obviously not what God wants. We spoke about various kinds of other addictions: food, exercise, porn, overworking etc. He felt happy that he was clear on this point, understood what it meant for his life and how to recognise it in the future.

He also pointed out that in my previous life in computers God didn't want that for me either. I acknowledged that was indeed the case, that corporate work and the 'yuppy' lifestyle, while good things in themselves, weren't good for me. They were taking me away from God, which I experienced as desolation. I pointed out how God works through everything, is in all experiences and, especially for me, was working through the experience of desolation to bring me to an awakening and a whole new search that eventually brought me to the Jesuits. I explained how God works with us, especially in our feelings, the interior life (God dwells within us, after all), and is always trying to steer us in a good direction.

Reflection point: Desolation is an uneasy feeling that invites doubts, fears, restlessness and temptation. We *feel* farthest away from God during this period, even though the opposite is true. The paradox is that desolation has a hidden message of alerting us to being on the wrong path and impelling

us to action. When these emotions of negativity, spiritual dryness and depression are
detected, we must act against the down-
ward spiral. Instead of passively waiting out
this 'storm' of negativity, Ignatius calls us
to take positive steps to move in the opposite direction and get back on track using
discernment.

Over dinner, I quoted Ignatius to James: 'Ingrati-
tude is the greatest sin and the root of all sin. It is,
in the end, the failure to love as God has loved us.'
I also sent him a copy of the five-step Ignatian Examen[15] that I wanted him to do every night, recom-
mending that he spend at least fifteen minutes on
it. I also added the Ignatian point that 'love shows
itself more in deeds than words', underlining the
importance of actions, decisions and concrete plans
for back home. We agreed that at the end of the
pilgrimage we would come up with a plan for him
to follow back home.

James repeated that he wanted to keep this good
experience going but was afraid of losing it on his
return. I again pointed out that that this fear was

---

15 https://jesuit.ie/blog/brendan-mcmanus/examen-the-paradox-of
    -reflection/.

not from God, and that he had to act against letting that negative thought dominate. He had to believe that he was created by God (therefore fundamentally good), that the spirit dwelled within him (a 'temple') and that God had only good things in store for him.

Reflection point: A fundamental starting point is accepting that we are created by God and that our happiness lies in following God's will. Through reflection and discernment we can uncover this 'divine GPS signal' inside ourselves and use it to make decisions. This is essentially a gift of God's love, freely given, that we can detect, discern and follow. This amounts to a 'felt sense' of being carried or held in compassionate love, which reflects our identity as 'creatures' (created by God). The good news is that this is always there for us and we are never abandoned. At any time we can receive this healing and help towards reintegration in becoming who we truly are.

Chapter 9

Rescued by Nuns

Right from the start nothing seemed to be working out that morning. We had arranged to have breakfast together at six o'clock, but when I arrived James was already halfway through his. By the time I had ordered coffee and a croissant, a man on crutches had sat in my seat and I had to stand at the bar with all the early morning truckers. I never needed a morning coffee more.

Our plan that day was to walk the relatively small stage of 15km into Igualada, but we didn't get too far before James was complaining about pain in his leg and saying that he wasn't going to be able to walk any further. Travelling the short distance back to where we had spent the previous night, we narrowly missed a local bus, and when we arrived at the motel we sat outside at a table to weigh up our options. There was one more bus in thirty minutes and then none till late afternoon, so we pinned all our hopes on that. However, when the Alda bus pulled in, the driver wouldn't let us on when we told him the destination. This was intensely irritating; I had the timetable on my phone with the stops and it seemed to be simply a capricious bus driver who was making things difficult for us.

With few other options, we sat down again, smarting from the refusal. This was a tough moment; the morning was slipping away from us as the sun climbed higher and turned up the heat. I was praying hard for help in this situation, asking for a way out of this hot and unpleasant place, a place we didn't want to be in, never mind spend another night in. We considered calling a taxi, which would have been very expensive on our depleted budget, but instead opted for trying to get a lift.

Reflection point: A key point is remembering to pray in difficult situations, especially when stress levels are high. The temptation is always to think that God has abandoned us; while this is plainly untrue, our emotions can dictate otherwise. The other crucial thing is to 'pray with the problem'; asking for help with an overwhelming situation helps to calm anxiety, reach for a higher power and be more open to options, that is, to make better decisions.

The waitress very kindly wrote us out a sign in Spanish for our destination, Igualada, and I reluctantly began to approach drivers and diners to see if they would take us. Most were kind but were either going in the wrong direction or couldn't take us because of company policy and insurance. A woman driver who took an interest in us explained that this truck stop was off the main route and that we would be better off at the roundabout a kilometre away. However, we knew that our only chance was to ask drivers face to face here.

After we had been there for a couple of long hours, James was growing disconsolate, although I was still hopeful and praying hard for some assistance. Then I saw some nuns in full habits alighting from a minibus. Inside, I approached them for a lift, explaining that I was a Jesuit and my friend, unable to walk, needed a lift. I was taken aback by the immediate positive response I got from the mother superior, whose name was Montserrat. Not only did they offer us a lift to Igualada, where they had to pick up another sister, but they were actually going on to Montserrat, our next day's destination. As they were having breakfast, we waited outside for them, marvelling at our good fortune and providence. Shortly afterwards, their driver pulled up in their minibus and we were all off to Igualada. Their residence there was an extraordinary building that resembled a castle, apparently designed by a Gaudí disciple. We had some photos taken there with them while they located the other sister who would also travel with us. They explained they were members of an order, Hermanitas de los Ancianos Desamparados (Little Sisters of the Forsaken Elderly).

On the way up the dramatic winding road to Montserrat, James insisted on singing 'Let it Be' for them. As they had never heard of the Beatles, I had to translate the lyrics and explain the significance of the song. For Catholics 'Mother Mary' is taken to mean the Virgin Mary, though apparently Paul McCartney was writing about his own mother, Mary.

Sister Montserrat's story

Montserrat was born in a small town in the province of Lleida called Gimenells. Her parents were simple people, farmers, and they lived the faith they had received from their parents. They gave her the name Montserrat because of her mother's devotion to the Blessed Virgin Mary and because they wanted their first daughter to bear the name of the patron saint of Catalonia.

When she was about six years old, some sisters would come to the house to ask for alms and food, and she was allowed accompany them through the town, sharing the little bread and provisions they brought. Even at school, when she was asked, 'What do you want to be when you grow up?', she always answered, 'I want to be a nun'. Then, at the age of ten, without telling her parents, she wrote to a religious school that an older friend attended, asking if she could go there too. Eventually a letter arrived for her parents from the school, and she had to tell them what had happened. To her surprise, they allowed her to go the next year.

This boarding school was run by the Congregation of the Little Sisters of the Forsaken Elderly, and she felt at home and very happy there, although she missed her family. After finishing school, she went directly into the postulancy programme and later took the habit of the congregation. In 1989 she made her perpetual profession, consecrating her life to God 'completely and for ever'. She has been very happy dedicating her skills and talents to the poor and helpless elderly, this often-forgotten sector of society in such need of love and tenderness to make present the closeness and love of God.

The road wound its way around the striking pink rock cliffs, giving glimpses of peaks and sheer drops. Rocks, gravel, sand and clay deposited by rivers millions of years ago had been elevated by shifts in the earth's plates, then sculpted and shaped by erosion to form Montserrat's curiously rounded pillars and bands of gradated rock. It spoke of powerful pressures, hidden processes and great transformations. Once again I had to marvel at this powerful site for a Benedictine monastery and for prayer and reflection. I could imagine Ignatius's awe on arriving here for the first time in 1622.

Arriving at the shrine of Montserrat (it literally means 'saw-toothed mountain'), we swept through the car park and barriers and, like dignitaries, were deposited right outside the imposing basilica at the heart of the shrine. We were just in time for midday mass and joined the sisters for the service. It was impossible not to be moved by the beautifully elegant Benedictine liturgy, the impressive sanctuary overlooked by the iconic Black Virgin statue, and the crowds that thronged the nave. I was feeling enormous gratitude for how we had got here, such a work of providence.

> **Reflection point:** Gratitude is key to the Examen prayer and to the whole Ignatian system, we realise how much we are loved and how close God is to us. This seeing everything as a gift comes from understanding how much we have received, and it opens our hearts to the world. The goal is continually to cultivate

an 'attitude of gratitude' that transforms every experience and, indeed, our lives.

After the mass we went to the pastoral centre and registered as pilgrims, and were given beds in the hostel and a voucher to get a reduced-price dinner at the evening buffet. We enjoyed a light lunch in the sunshine in the plaza outside the hostel, in what was to become our spot to hang out and watch the hordes of pilgrims and tourists passing through. I was very touched that James, without consulting me, negotiated with the hostel warden to get me a separate bunk room where I could pray and reflect. We passed an enjoyable evening resting in our bunks, savouring the all-you-can-eat buffet, and watching the sun go down over the marvel that was Montserrat.

Reflection point: The Benedictine shrine to Our Lady of Montserrat, with its venerated statue of the Black Madonna and Child, was where Ignatius realised some key aspects of his transformation. Handing over his sword and dagger during a dramatic all-night vigil at the altar of Our Lady, he committed himself to Christ, his new Lord. Then, dressed in sackcloth like a beggar, he cast off his old life. Even though the process was to last many

years, this was an important moment of ritual, symbol and prayer in a key Catalonian
pilgrimage site. Likewise, we need moments
of religious ritual in our lives of commitment
and transformation.

Chapter 10

A Meeting of Minds and Hearts

Waking early, as was my custom, I set out on one of the many walks around Montserrat. I first picked up the *Via Crucis*, or Way of the Cross, which served as a morning meditation. The stations depicting the last hours of Jesus' life seemed to speak to me about the depths of the love that Christ has for me personally. Then I picked up the trail to St Michael's Cross, located on a dramatic ridge jutting out from the mountain, which offers some of the best views of the shrine and the valley below. The rising sun bathed the scene in an ethereal light that brought a lump to my throat. Overwhelmed by such beauty, I had to sit down and contemplate the vista with much gratitude. I returned, brimming with the grace I had received gratuitously, as the complex was springing into life. A worker hosing down the pavements almost soaked me as I emerged onto the plaza. It was going to be a great day, which we had decided to spend savouring Montserrat.

Reflection point: Contemplation is simply being present to the wonder of everyday scenes, especially in nature, which always reflects something of God. The problem is often that we don't see things the way they are, but rather as we are, and so it's about clearing our emotions and perceptions to be open to the 'real'. Ignatius used to get great consolation from simply gazing at the stars at night. Our challenge is to develop these same ways of looking in order to see what is really there (God is in the 'real').

This extra day in Montserrat would be a quiet reflective day, which was appropriate in this special mountain retreat. To begin the day, I sent James a morning prayer by Jesuit John Veltri:

O God, I find myself at the beginning of
    another day.
I do not know what it will bring.
Please help me to be ready for whatever it
    may be.
If I am to stand up, help me to stand bravely.
If I am to sit still, help me to sit quietly.
If I am to lie low, help me to do it patiently.
If I am to do nothing, let me do it gallantly.

I pray just for today, for these twenty-four
  hours,
for the ability to cooperate with others
  according to
the way Jesus taught us to live.
'Your kingdom come, your will be done on
  earth as it is in heaven.'
May these words that he taught us become
  more than words.
Please free my thinking and feelings and
the thinking and feelings of others, from all
forms of self-will, self-centredness, dishon-
esty and deception. Along with my brothers
and sisters, I need this freedom to make
my choices today according to your desires.
Send your Spirit to inspire me in time of
doubt and indecision so that, together, we
can walk along your path. Amen.

We attended the magnificent Benedictine liturgy
at eleven that morning, when I was privileged to
concelebrate at the mass. This was made even more
special as it was the ordination of one of the young
Benedictine monks and the church was packed with
relatives and friends as well as the normal throng
of pilgrims. It was special to be in the choir stalls
among the monks during the sung mass, including

the Ave Maria, and looking out I found James in the congregation, standing at the wall as he'd given up his seat for someone else. I was conscious of the statue of the Black Madonna above me, the famous effigy of Our Lady that had drawn pilgrims for centuries, including Ignatius Loyola with his profound Marian devotion.

> **Reflection point:** Devotion to Mary played a key role in the life and vocation of Ignatius, culminating in his conversion. His devotion to the Virgin Mary was a theme that connected many of the pilgrimage places along this route: Arantzazu, Navarrete and Montserrat. Certainly, his special devotion to Mary on the way to Montserrat helped protect him from falling back into his old habits and attachments. Mary can be seen helpfully as the 'perfect apostle' who always follows the Spirit, the epitome of Ignatian freedom.

Afterwards we had a simple lunch in the Plaza de L'Abat Oliva in front of our hostel. Crowds of pilgrims, group guides and tourists milled around on their way to the abbey church. It was a festive atmosphere, helped by the dramatic mountain scenery and the beautiful weather. Fortunately, the altitude took the edge off the intense heat, and it was pleasant to stroll around for a change. I encouraged James to seek out confession, knowing that Ignatius had made a full confession and left his old life behind here. I took a reflective moment alone at a coffee shop to try to write some lines on our journey:

> Sun blasted
> Heat treated
> Still dehydrated
> Washed out
> Heat rashed
> Sore legs
> Tested in the fire
> Reshaped in the furnace.
>
> Delivered from the desert
> Deeply consoled
> Slightly insightful
> Spent, worn out
> Dusty shoes
> Dirt of the trail
> Severely tested.

In the afternoon I took the St Joan funicular up into the high mountain peaks to walk a bit and to explore some of the old hermitages I had heard about. Apparently, Ignatius had come up here to visit some of the hermits who lived on the side of the mountain. It was another hot day and the afternoon sun was intense with little shade around. I encountered only small numbers of tourists on the path, which has spectacular views and vertiginous drops on one side. I turned off and took the rough trail for St Magdelena's hermitage, which led directly up into the towering peaks. I passed a whole series of ruined hermitages spread out over the mountain and the path wove in and out through overhangs, tunnels and vertical stone staircases. The outline of the ruined hermitage in a shady glade was all that remained, but it was enough to conjure an image of the lifestyle and lofty isolation of this mountain retreat. I took some time to sit and reflect about how important this place had been for Ignatius, how he had dramatically divested himself of his old life, hanging up his dagger and sword, and keeping an all-night vigil (which I had tried unsuccessfully to imitate in 2015). I also prayed for James on his journey and for my role as his spiritual guide.

Reflection point: Montserrat is important for Ignatius in that he receives guidance from a French monk, Fr Jean Chanon, and learns the value of having a mentor and a spiritual guide. He then builds this into the Spiritual Exercises in terms of the key role of the spiritual director as guide: the person actively listening to help the other find freedom and to choose well. Spiritual direction offers a companion for the spiritual journey, a guide who can more easily spot the movements and unfreedoms. Spiritual directors actively listen, helping people to find freedom, make balanced decisions and grow closer to God.

Later that afternoon, I explained to James the famous Ignatian meditation on the 'Three types of Person' and how it was linked to the Ignatian concept of freedom and discernment. Now that we were nearing the end, I wanted James to begin thinking about his going home and how he would integrate his new insights about faith and life.

In the Spiritual Exercises Ignatius proposes an imaginary exercise about three people's different approaches to having acquired a great sum of money. They are faced with the dilemma of figuring out what God wants them to do with it (*Spiritual Exercises*, 149–156). Will they be able to take it to God or will they be overly attached to the money? The exercise is a test of the person's freedom or detachment so as to see how deep or integrated their faith is. The three types of people are caricatures: the procrastinator, the compromiser/dealer and the 'free' person.

1. The first type procrastinates, postponing what they know they should do. They want to become free of the attachment to the money, but they never take the means necessary to achieve that freedom. They remain attached to it and are 'unfree' in their inaction.

2. The second type knows what they should do but they compromise or make a deal about what to do with the money. In what seems like a virtuous act, they allocate some of the money for others, but they hold something back for themselves. Though there is something of God in their desire to be free, they still cannot let go of their attachment; they 'make a deal' with God that reveals their priority in maintaining control and so they are 'unfree'.

3. The third type of person wants to be free to respond to what God asks, they want to be 'indifferent' and open to using or not using the money. Significantly, their desire is to

do what God wants, and in this consists real freedom.

I asked James to reflect on this exercise as to where he would place himself.

In the evening, while we were waiting for the opening of the hostel buffet, which featured a discounted pilgrim menu, James went outside for some air. A very sociable creature, he had this amazing knack for meeting people and making friends. On his return, he introduced me to a family group who came from near Barcelona. The father, Manuel, was Spanish, while the mother, Lorraine was Irish, and they had two adorable kids, Matthew (came to her in a dream) and Nieves-Cara (from 'anam cara', soul friend in Irish). They had to rush off to feed the children just then but agreed to meet us afterwards outside in the plaza.

Now, after dinner, as the day trippers started to thin out, we had the Plaza de L'Abat Oliva largely to ourselves. A convenient bench was fast becoming our base for hanging out and meeting people and we got to talking with the family right away. It was one of those Camino moments where we just connected, having so much in common as pilgrims here in Montserrat. James and I explained our pilgrimage journey and the retreat we had been on together, telling the stories of providence and making it through. Inevitably, our conversation turned to matters of the heart, God and meaning, how we were making sense of our life journeys. We had much in common and exchanged viewpoints animatedly.

Reflection point: Spiritual conversation is a dialogue between friends about life and meaning. Ignatius practised this in his many pilgrim encounters, being an open ear to listen to where people were at and offering his own experience and insights about God. This is something that happens naturally in any meaningful conversation, as friendship and trust develop and dialogue gets deeper and turns to significant life issues and questions. Rather than a debate, it is a mutual sharing of viewpoints and insights, where no one seeks to 'win', as such, but rather both parties are enriched through dialogue. This is where God is, in the desires and yearnings of our hearts, and we recognise and appreciate others, especially where there is a real meeting of minds and hearts that enriches both.

I found Manuel in particular very engaging, and his background in philosophy and spirituality made for riveting conversation between us. We must have spent several hours chatting until it got dark and cool, and the kids started to get tired. It was a magical evening as we just connected, talking about spirituality and life, all the really important things, in true pilgrim fashion.

Manuel's story

Manuel first studied engineering in Barcelona and then went to Ireland to carry out his final degree project. He met Lorraine there. During almost seven years in Ireland, he worked in various international companies as an engineer and then began studying for a master's degree in sustainable development, where he discovered his interests lay beyond engineering. He lived and worked on projects in sustainability in Ireland, the UK, Norway and Spain, which involved working on projects in Europe, Latin America and Africa. His dream was to create a more balanced society and a better world, and he began to look for a project with more meaning and imagination.

He quickly realised the need for philosophical reflection in his own daily life and worked with Spanish academic professionals, including Dr. Octavi Piulats at the University of Barcelona. He combined philosophy, self-knowledge and spirituality in his master's thesis, going on to do a PhD in the study of the self and sustainable development. He works in project development and corporate ethics, while lecturing at different levels, regularly focusing on people from disadvantaged backgrounds.

Manuel likes conversation and exchange, realising how personal encounters can become significant and life changing. He has walked the Camino de Santiago and realised its potential for personal growth through conversation as well as silence, and especially through contact with nature. Manuel is a regular visitor to Montserrat, which he sees as a sacred place with a long tradition and the intersection of different traditions. We have kept in touch over his interest in reflection, consciousness and integrating life and action through the Ignatian method.

Chapter 11

Making it to Manresa: The Last Day

A beautiful morning sky over Montserrat found me out early walking on a trail up to the *mirador*, or look-out. I passed a group silently meditating as the sun rose, radiant silhouettes against the sun. Shortly afterwards, I found a lofty spot to sit alone and watch the beauty unfold. The sun seemed to bring out a honey glow in the rocks, and the abbey church complex, initially in shadow, sprang into relief. The towering rock pillars all around dwarfed the now tiny buildings, clinging precariously to the sheer faces. The poignancy was that this was our last day in Montserrat and the last day of our pilgrimage as we would arrive in Manresa later that afternoon. As always, it was a bittersweet feeling: experiencing the thrill of being a pilgrim on the road alongside the desire for rest and shelter from the endless heat.

I sent James this excerpt from an email that had just arrived in my inbox from Richard Rohr in relation to AA and 'emotional sobriety'. It perfectly described Ignatian freedom or 'detachment' from emotions or passions, which we had been discussing some days before in relation to his difficult experience in Zaragoza:

> Much of the work of emotional maturity is learning to distinguish between emotions that offer a helpful message about ourselves or the moment, and emotions that are merely narcissistic reactions to the moment. I dare to say that, until we have found our spiritual center and ground, most of our emotional responses are usually too self-referential to be helpful or truthful. They read the moment as if the 'I,' with its immediate needs and hurts, is the reference point for objective truth. It isn't. The small, defensive 'I' cannot hold that space. Reality/God/Creation holds that space. Persistent use of the small self as an objective reference point will only create deeper problems in the long run; it will not solve them.[16]

---

16 Adapted from Richard Rohr, *Emotional Sobriety: Rewiring Our Programs for 'Happiness'*, https://cac.org/daily-meditations/emotional -maturity-2022-06-19/.

I was reflecting how far James had come and how I had seen him grow on this pilgrimage and retreat we had done together. He had benefitted greatly from the AA programme, had turned his life and relationships around as a result, and had been sober for over ten years at this point. What he was learning from Ignatius was the fine tuning of faith, being more aware of situations and emotions. He had learned a lot about reflection, the ability to step back from a situation and examine the emotions, motivations and possible choices involved. Realising that there was often no standard or stock response that could be used, he was conscious of the uniqueness of situations and how each one had to be examined carefully. He was growing in discernment, the wisdom of being more self-aware, and tuned in to different situations that required individual responses. He was better able to come up with wise choices and actions that were more Spirit led. I was confident we would be able to handle situations differently.

Reflection point: One of Ignatius's fundamental insights in the Spiritual Exercises was that God deals with each of us uniquely, in the particular mix of strengths and weaknesses that we bring when we have to negotiate an individual path. Self-knowledge, awareness and reflection, as well as having a spiritual guide, help to sift emotions and judge which ones are genuine. The goal is to become free from any undue influence, poised like the midpoint of a balance, in order to decide and act well. Ignatius invites us to face our fears, make discerned decisions, and act against unhealthy attachments. This takes courage, honesty and a radical dependence on God. Our moods and inner feelings are useful in recognising destructive impulses and distinguishing them from those that are genuinely life-giving.

Arriving back at the hostel, we packed quickly and went down to wait for the first funicular down the mountain at 8.15. As we ate our breakfast sandwiches at a table outside, the only people passing were a few serious climbers swathed in ropes. I saw a man waiting at the station whom I recognised from the previous night. He had asked me for help in getting into the hostel. To my surprise, he said he was also going to Manresa as he was looking for a Jesuit priest. Intrigued, I told him that I was one. He explained that he was an inventor and had these brilliant ideas on ecological technology that would 'save the world', but no one would listen to him. We had a very intense discussion before the funicular left, trying to get to the bottom of what his problem was. He acknowledged that he was unhappy and he certainly looked sad. He had a daughter and was divorced. He seemed very intelligent and resourceful, though poorly dressed. He certainly had a passion for science and inventions and was largely self-taught, with his own workshop.

In spiritual director mode, I was trying to explore how I could help him. I launched into an imaginary painting, a picture of extremes: I asked him to imagine one person who is driven and obsessed in working on something, and then another who is disengaged and not using their talents. However, he was quick to deny that there was any issue of extremes in his life. Next, I tried the idea of 'channelling the inner fire',[17] that we are instruments for the power of God working through us, and introduced the idea of good and bad: given that we can collaborate with the life of the spirit, certain actions are helpful and 'good', and others unhelpful and 'bad'. Again, he quickly wrote off the idea that there

17 After my booklet of the same name: https://www.messenger.ie /product/channelling-the-inner-fire-ignatian-spirituality-in-15 -points/.

was any 'bad' working in him. I was surprised at this, and my 'radar' was telling me that the poor man was trapped somehow. It could have been some kind of technological obsession, or something much deeper, but I was sad that I couldn't help him more.

However, time was running out as the funicular departure was imminent and I had to run to the station where James was waiting for me. I gave the man my business card and offered to meet him in Manresa so that we could talk more. I heard later that he did go to the Jesuit Centre in Manresa and had asked for a Jesuit priest to talk to, so I hope that he got some assistance.

Reflection point: The role of a spiritual director or guide is to help people to come to some awareness or insight about their lives through asking questions. An essential starting point is that we are created by God and given gifts and talents, and that our joy consists in using those fully (consolation). However, we also have a tendency to squander these, or get caught up in ideology, attachments or traps that make us less human or disconnected (desolation). We can often be misled in seemingly good things

113

('I have a unique contribution to make'),
which blinds us to their destructive conse-
quences (isolation and disconnection). This
is known as the 'Angel of Light Deception',
and it describes how we become enslaved to
ideas and compulsions. Refusing to accept
our basic humanity and 'creaturehood' (I
am the dependent creature, not the creator)
blocks the process and makes progress difficult or impossible.

After a winding descent of spectacular views, all
three of us transferred to the train to Manresa. As
James still wasn't up to walking, I had to make sure
he got the train to Manresa, where I had arranged
for my Jesuit friend Devadhas to meet him. However, I planned to get off halfway and walk the last
15km as a symbolic gesture. Therefore, I got off the
train in Sant Vincenç de Castellet, planning to get
a bus or taxi across to the nearby town of Castellgali, which would put me back on the Camino. I
headed into town and asked some women where
the centre was. An older woman with a kindly face
initially gave me directions and then decided to
take me there herself. As we walked together, she
greeted lots of people she knew and asked them
on my behalf about how to get to Castellgali. One

friend she met recommended getting the train as the station was close. I headed for the station and, consulting my phone along the way, realised that there was no train connection. I retraced my steps to the main plaza and considered my options. I asked around for a taxi but no one seemed to know of one, and I also checked out a bus but that didn't go for an hour or so. I was conscious of the time as I had arranged to meet Devadhas and James on the outskirts of Manresa for the final walk in.

Finding myself getting agitated over these arrangements that didn't seem to be working out, I bought a coffee and took a moment to sit back and reflect. Ironically, I still had a train ticket to Manresa in my pocket and, laughing to myself, I realised that the easiest thing was simply to get back on the train, make the short walk to the rendezvous point, and meet my friends as arranged. Having taken all the pressure off I enjoyed my coffee and the shady plaza. I thought it an ironic and appropriate finale to this unpredictable and serendipitous pilgrimage; 'just let go and enjoy', I thought, appreciating the moment.

Reflection point: One of the key Ignatian practices is that of reflection and awareness, simply tuning in to the reality around us. Sometimes the solution is right under our noses and time and space are required for it to emerge. We can easily get trapped in expectations, unrealistic plans and 'ideas of perfection'. Often, we need to break the unhelpful dynamics of rushing and driving ourselves hard; this needs a courageous 'acting against' the desolation and changing the dynamics. It's all about letting go of control, being humble and flexible enough to change plans and finding peace and consolation.

An hour later I was slowly walking out from Manresa in the baking heat to our rendezvous point at the Torre de Santa Caterina, which has a dramatic view over the Cardoner river valley, the Manresa retreat house and the Seu cathedral. This was the same place that I had frequented as part of my Ignatian course a month beforehand and where I had trained for the Camino, and so it was a fitting meeting place. I was early and found a rock to sit on in the shade, reflecting on all that had happened up to this point. I was feeling a mixture of gratitude and also relief at finishing; it had been challenging and unexpectedly demanding, especially with the unprecedented heat. I could see my two friends, James and Devadhas, deep in conversation, approaching me on the path. It was an emotional meeting, the final walk in made more poignant by the fact that Devadhas, stuck in Manresa waiting for a visa, had several health issues that made walking difficult. The last kilometre, past La Guía chapel, over the Roman bridge, under La Seu cathedral, was directly in the footsteps of Ignatius who had arrived 500 years earlier.

We slowly walked the last few kilometres and paused on the steps of the retreat house. James was in triumphant mood, delighted at having made it to the place he so wanted to visit. For Devadhas and myself, it was a coming home to the Jesuit retreat house where we had spent several happy weeks together. Personally, I was glad to be getting out of the heat and eagerly anticipating air conditioning and a cool room.

Devadhas's story

Devadhas was born in Rajavoor, a village in Tamil Nadu state, in the southern part of India. At the age of four he sneaked into a mass in Latin. When the priest said 'Ite missa est' for the end of mass, Devadhas inadvertently let out a whistle of admiration and then took to his heels. The priest chased after him and made him kneel in front of the Blessed Sacrament. He credits that as the day he decided to become a priest.

Even at the young age of fifteen he was giving the other seminarians in his class advice about how to be like Jesus; they should welcome everyone and exclude no one. He joined the Society of Jesus in 1971 but found the novitiate difficult; even though he was pious he was very talkative and couldn't keep the silence. During his philosophy in Pune, he knew all the 183 Jesuit scholastics by name and had great friendships. Once he was asked to leave the Society for being too emotional but his spiritual guide interceded on his behalf and he stayed.

He was ordained a priest in 1984 and initially assigned to a boarding school as a teacher. Being from a poor background himself, he always favoured the poorer students, but this did not always please the management. Eventually, he had to resign and joined the Jesuit Refugee Service, working for Caritas Nepal. He worked with Bhutanese refugees there for two years and was then asked to go to Zimbabwe as a missionary, serving in Harare for two and a half years. He was then called back to the Province and served again in schools for the Dalits or outcasts, and led preached retreats. Cardiac issues led to triple bypass surgery in 2009, and he credits his recovery to a vision of Mother Mary and her Son

*Jesus on the Cross. His desire to deepen his understand-
ing of Ignatian spirituality brought him to Manresa in
Spain, where he and I were classmates.*

That evening James, Devadhas and I celebrated
mass together in the famous Cave of Ignatius, a
chapel made from rock. It was a poignant moment,
being in the place where Ignatius had prayed and
reputedly worked on his famous Spiritual Exercises.
It was a big moment, especially for James, the end
of the pilgrimage and his first time in the cave, and
I could see that he was deeply moved. At the beginning of mass, he took out all sorts of memorial
cards, photos and rosary beads and arranged them
around the altar, mementos of his prayer intentions
and his journey. The readings of the Sunday vigil
mass were appropriate: Elijah's calling of Elisha (1
Kings 19), 'You show me the path of life' (Psalm
15), 'Led by the Spirit' (Galatians 5), and Jesus' calling of the disciples (Luke 9).

In my short homily I summarised the journey that
James and myself had been on together in terms of
these 'journey' themes:

- Our overwhelming emotion was gratitude for
all that Christ had done for us, especially how

we had been kept safe during the severe heat and found a way through the 'desert' (kept safe while *'walking through fire'*, Isaiah 43:2).

- We had been redeemed and restored; it was a testing time with many challenges, and we had come to know God better and had grown in faith.

- Just as it was for Ignatius, the journey to Manresa had been a time of deepening and purifying faith; we had learned about discernment, true freedom and making wise decisions.

- Given all that we had learned, we had a profound sense of providence working through all the people we had come into contact with.

- We understood better what it was to be pilgrims like Ignatius, travelling light (Luke 9:3), being flexible and just wanting to do the Father's will.

- Especially, we had learned about Ignatian freedom, getting free of unhealthy attachments, and always discerning God's will.

- Returning home, we wanted to be instruments of God in our world, in relationships and for our families and friends, and to be of service to others.

Finally, Devadhas added that 'self-emptying' is what James had talked to him about that morning on the walk. He captured the theme, addressing James directly: 'He has to empty himself so that God can fill him! He has become most Ignatian.' Later we got our pilgrim passports stamped and I presented James with his pilgrim certificate on the terrace in the evening light looking out on the lights of Manresa. James played me his favourite Dire Straits song, 'Going Home'. It was the perfect ending.

Epilogue

Before James and I left Manresa, we took a day to reflect on the whole experience using the questions in the Appendix below, and then had a final conversation to integrate all that we had learned and the insights we had gained.

I explained to James how Ignatius was not made in one moment at Loyola (the unhelpful 'miraculous conversion' idea); it took many months and even years on the road to sort out his own issues and excesses. Full of wilfulness and ego initially ('all the great things I do for God'), he had to arrive at the end of his own strength and abilities to let God in. He had to learn about who God really was – loving compassion and not judgement – and learn how to relate in a life-giving and balanced way, as he had damaged his health with all his extremes. I explained that the Manresa experience in particular was the deepening and purification of his faith, the ironing out of wrinkles, the refining of his process and then formulation of it for others in the Spiritual Exercises and retreats. We also spoke of the vision he had at the Cardoner River, how this was an integrating moment of great awareness of God in all things and all things in God. There was an immediate and accessible intimacy that changed the way Ignatius lived and breathed his faith. There was no more appropriate place to reflect together on our pilgrimage and the same issues.

I lit a candle and read Psalm 15, the Righteous Israelite, which seemed to describe James. We then reviewed the questions in terms of these Ignatian themes:

1. We are created by God and given gifts and talents for life's journey (fundamental goodness).

2. We have a tendency to forget this, to make mistakes, but God always gives us a way back (the reality of sin and forgiveness).

3. God is always with us, and can be seen especially when looking back on our life journey (the importance of reflection, 'retreating' and getting perspective).

4. The story of Ignatius Loyola in his dictated autobiography is really helpful as it maps out his faith journey for us in all its ups and downs; walking in his footsteps helps us to relive the experience and get some of the insights.

5. God is especially with us in those moments of difficulty or obstacles (the Cross) in our lives;

often these moments of darkness or great suffering are a purification and a 'testing in the fire' that allow us to face our demons and humbly find a way forward with God's help (handing over control and trusting).

6. God is close to us and in constant relationship with us, but we have to do our part, walk our road of faith as best we can.

7. Prayer has to be a dialogue; there has to be speaking, petitioning and imploring, but also listening, reflecting and discerning/acting. The challenge is to be attentive to the urgings of the Spirit and to follow them.

8. God works in our interior moods and feelings, and we can pick up those internal movements of consolation and desolation to find where God is leading (the importance of discernment).

9. Our job is to be collaborators or instruments of God's compassion in the world, to help others and to give something back (to be of service in building a better world).

10. We need to structure our lives to make sure that we have prayer and reflection built in so that we can remain close to God (putting good habits and structures in place).

11. The hardest things are freedom and humility, the letting go of control. We need to trust that God is in charge and know that it is not up to us.

**My suggestions for James when
he went home were:**

1. Do the full Examen at the end of each day, taking about fifteen minutes to review the day and see where you've been with God, or not: https://www.ignatianspirituality.com/the-steps-of-the-examen/amp/.

2. Pray each day for at least fifteen minutes. Remember that prayer is also listening, so create a space and maybe use scripture to hear what God is saying to you. I recommend Sacred Space on your phone: https://www.sacredspace.ie.

3. Take time to discern and pray about decisions, especially important ones; no quick, rushed decisions: https://www.ignatianspirituality.com/making-good-decisions/an-approach-to-good-choices/an-ignatian-framework-for-making-a-decision/?amp.

4. Try to be the person God wants you to be, treating others well, having good healthy relationships and having a goal/direction in life. Try to help others whenever you can.

5. Think about having a spiritual director or some-one to whom you can talk regularly about faith.

6. Keep a spiritual diary or notebook (just like Ignatius) to record important events and help you reflect on them: https://www.ignatianspirituality .com/ignatian-prayer/the-what-how-why-of-prayer /review-prayer-by-keeping-a-journal/?amp.

7. Think about doing a retreat or spiritual Camino walk once a year to keep on track. Find a local retreat centre that can help you.

8. Keep up some sort of spiritual reading to keep your faith life alive, especially Ignatian books: https:// www.goodreads.com/shelf/show/jesuit-spirituality.

Appendix: Pilgrimage Reflection Questions

As with any important experience, it is good to reflect on it afterwards. These questions are suggested as an aid to your reflection on the pilgrimage. You may like to write a private diary or journal to help you process the experience.

1. How did you come to the pilgrimage, and what frame of mind were you starting out with? How did the pilgrimage change you, if at all?

2. Did anything stop you from giving yourself fully to the experience?

3. What memories stand out for you? What image or metaphor captures the experience for you?

4. What were the high points for you?

5. What were the low points for you?

6. Were there any moments of the 'Cross', suffering, darkness or difficulty? Did you sense Christ's presence in these (maybe afterwards)? Were you able to pray with them?

7. Was there any place/person/experience where you particularly felt the presence of God? Where did you feel that God was speaking to you?

8. What have you learned about yourself? What have you learned about God?

9. What will you do differently after this pilgrimage? How, if at all, has it changed your life? What concrete decisions, if any, emerged from the pilgrimage?

10. Is there anything you still need to do? What changes would help you to stay in consolation?

Music Playlist

(available on the author's Spotify account with this link: shorturl.at/dgQ89, or the author's public Facebook page: www.facebook.com/BrendanSJ)

1. 'Perfect Day', Lou Reed
2. 'The Sound of Silence', Simon and Garfunkel
3. 'You've Got a Friend', James Taylor
4. 'On the Road Again', Canned Heat
5. 'The Heat is On', Glenn Frey
6. 'Brothers in Arms', Dire Straits
7. 'Amazing Grace', Aretha Franklin
8. 'Radio', The Corrs
9. 'Let it Be', The Beatles
10. 'Ave Maria', Benedictine Monks
11. 'Going Home', Dire Straits

Acknowledgements

- The wonderful and talented James Fullam, who was a great companion and friend on this journey.
- The Belfast Jesuit Community and Irish Jesuit Province, who supported me on this pilgrimage, my family and friends.
- Jose Luis Iriberri SJ, Director of the Camino Ignaciano, who briefed me initially and then did a debrief with us afterwards.
- Director Javier Melloni SJ and the staff of La Cova Spirituality Centre, Manresa, who supported and looked after us so well.
- Jose Ignacio Clavero Rodriguez, who provided much support and made contact with Anna Maria Pijuan.
- Anna Maria Pijuan, our wonderful tour guide in Verdú, and also the woman from the tourist office there.
- My friend Fr Colin Crossey, who presided at my uncle's funeral.

- Abbess Montserrat and the Hermanitas de los Ancianos Desamparados, who gave us that crucial lift to Montserrat.
- Jordi, who received us in the Montserrat Pastoral Centre.
- Logroño Jesuit Community, who looked after me so well.
- David Fagundo SJ and the Zaragoza Jesuit Community, who welcomed me so warmly
- Lleida Jesuit Community and Superior Alexis Bueno Guinamard, who received us so warmly and hosted an evening of songs.
- La Cova Manresa Spirituality Centre, who hosted us after the walk for the debrief and for writing this book.
- Padre José Gracia from Pina de Ebro, who received me so warmly in his church, gave me a lift to Bujaraloz where James was waiting, and prayed for us all along the way.
- On behalf of James I would like to thank his wife, Violet, four children and grandchildren for all their inspiration and support, especially his nephew David Farrell, who accompanied him on the first leg. Also the Irish 5th Infantry Battalion Veterans Committee and members for their support, and Catriona Fogarty for her help in promoting his walks, and to all those who donated to his charities.

Select Bibliography

David L. Fleming, *Draw Me into Your Friendship—The Spiritual Exercises: A Literal Translation and a Contemporary Reading*, St Louis, MO: Institute of Jesuit Sources, 1996.

José Luis Iriberri and Chris Lowney, *Guide to the Camino Ignaciano*, Bilbao: Ediciones Menajero, 3rd Edition, 2016.

Brendan McManus SJ, *Channelling the Inner Fire*, Dublin: Messenger Publications, 2022.

Brendan McManus SJ, *The Way to Manresa*, Dublin: Messenger Publications, 2021.

Brendan McManus SJ & Jim Deeds, *Discover God Daily: Seven Life-Changing Moments from the Journey of St Ignatius*, Dublin: Messenger Publications, 2022.

Brendan McManus SJ and Jim Deeds, *Finding God in the Mess: Meditations for Mindful Living*, Dublin: Messenger Publications, 2023 (revised edition).

Octavi Piulats, *Goethe y Montserrat* (Chapter 1, on Ignatius Loyola in Montserrat), Solsona: Solsona Comunicacions, 2001.

Juan Plazaola, *Ignatian Highways*, Assoc. Loila '91, 1990.

Joseph N. Tylenda, *A Pilgrim's Journey: The Autobiography of Ignatius of Loyola*, Collegeville, MN: Liturgical Press, 1991.